W9-BFF-891

#3

MathLand.

Journeys Through Mathematics

SKILL POWER

Essential

Practice

for

Every

Day

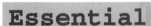

actice

ving

actice

ry

Creative Publications®

Writers
Julie Pier Brodie
Rhea Irvine
Cynthia Reak
Ann Roper
Sheri Rutman
Kelly Stewart
Kathryn Walker
Karie Youngdahl

Project Editors
Jo Dennis
Cynthia Reak
Andy Strauss
Kristin Ferraioli

Editors
Lynn Sanchez
Michelle Zachlod

Cover Design
Joslyn Hidalgo

Production Coordinator
Ed Lazar

Editorial Development
Pubworks

Production
Morgan-Cain & Associates

Portions of this book were previously published
under the title *Daily Tune-Ups II*.

©1998 Creative Publications
1300 Villa Street
Mountain View, CA 94041
Printed in the United States of America
ISBN 0-7622-0444-3
3 4 5 6 7 8 9 10. 03 02 01 00 99 98 97

Contents

Guidebook Unit	Focus	Introduction	Vocabulary	Race to the Finish	Follow the Trail	What's My Rule?	Problems	Test Practice
1	Data	1	2, 3	8 13, 14			4-7 9-12	
2	Equations	15	16, 17	22, 27 32, 37 42			18-21, 23-26 28-31, 33-36 38-41	
3	Patterns	43	44, 45	50 55, 56			46-49, 51-54	
4	Strategies	57	58, 59	64, 69	74 79, 84		60-63, 65-68 70-73, 75-78 80-83	
5	Logic	85	86, 87		92 97, 98		88-91, 93-96	
6	Number Groups	99	100, 101		106, 111 116, 121 126		102-105, 107-110 112-115, 117-120 122-125	
7	Measurements	127	128, 129		134, 139	144	130-133, 135-138 140-143	
8	Number Relations	145	146, 147			152, 157 162, 167 172	148-151, 153-156 158-161, 163-166 168-171	
9	Geometry	173	174, 175			180 185, 190	176-179, 181-184 186-189	
10	Probability	191	192, 193			198, 203 204, 205	194-197, 199-202	
	The Parade							206-215
	A Trip to the Nature Center							216-225

Skill Power Correlation / MathLand Guidebook

Unit	wk	pages	Investigation Focus	Skill Power pages	Vocabulary	Whole Number Operations +	Whole Number Operations −	Whole Number Operations ×	Whole Number Operations ÷	Number Combinations	Time	Money	Estimation	Problem Solving	Geometry	Logic	Grids/Graphs/Data Analysis	Algebra	Probability	Measurement	Patterns & Functions	Practice Tests
Unit 1 All About Us	1	6-13	Collecting Data	2-8	•	•	•	•			•	•		•		•		•			•	
	2	14-21	Reporting Datas	9-14		•	•	•		•	•	•		•		•	•					
Unit 2 Equations	1	30-37	Addition Equations	16-22	•	•	•			•		•		•		•	•	•			•	
	2	38-45	Subtraction Equations	23-27		•	•			•	•	•		•	•	•	•	•			•	
	3	46-53	Combination Patterns	28-32		•	•	•	•	•		•		•		•	•	•			•	
	4	54-61	Combinations for Ten	33-37		•	•			•		•		•		•		•			•	
	5	62-69	Math Stories	38-42		•	•		•	•	•	•		•		•	•	•			•	
Unit 3 Making Predictions	1	78-85	Predicting	44-50	•	•	•			•		•		•		•	•	•			•	
	2	86-93	2-Dimensional Patterns	51-56		•	•			•	•	•		•		•	•	•			•	
Unit 4 Strategies	1	102-109	Addition Equations	58-64		•	•		•	•		•		•		•	•	•			•	
	2	110-117	Related Equations	65-69	•	•	•			•		•		•		•		•			•	
	3	118-125	Memorization	70-74		•	•			•		•		•		•		•			•	
	4	126-133	Problem-Solving	75-79		•	•	•	•	•	•	•		•		•	•	•			•	
	5	134-141	Money Problems	80-84		•	•	•		•		•		•		•		•			•	
Unit 5 Collections	1	150-159	Classification	86-92	•	•	•	•	•	•	•	•		•		•	•	•			•	
	2	158-165	Organized Thinking	93-98		•	•	•	•	•	•	•		•		•	•	•			•	

Skill Power Correlation / MathLand Guidebook

Unit	wk	pages	Investigation Focus	Skill Power pages	Vocabulary	Whole Number Operations +	Whole Number Operations −	Whole Number Operations ×	Whole Number Operations ÷	Number Combinations	Time	Money	Estimation	Problem Solving	Geometry	Logic	Grids/Graphs/Data Analysis	Algebra	Probability	Measurement	Patterns & Functions	Practice Tests
Unit 6 Making Groups	1	174–181	Numbers 1–100	100–106	•	•	•	•		•	•		•	•		•	•	•		•	•	
	2	182–189	100-Number Patterns	107–111		•	•	•	•	•	•	•		•		•	•	•			•	
	3	190–197	Ordering	112–116		•	•	•		•		•	•	•		•	•	•			•	
	4	198–205	Measuring	117–121		•	•	•	•	•	•	•		•		•	•	•			•	
	5	206–213	Beyond 100	122–126		•	•	•		•	•	•		•		•	•	•			•	
Unit 7 How Long?	1	222–229	Length and Width	128–134	•	•	•	•		•		•	•	•		•	•	•		•	•	
	2	230–237	Solving Puzzles	135–139			•			•	•	•		•	•	•	•	•			•	
	3	238–245	Standard Units	140–144		•		•	•	•	•	•	•	•		•	•	•			•	
Unit 8 Expanding Number Relations	1	254–261	2-Digit Numbers	146–152	•	•	•	•		•		•		•	•	•		•			•	
	2	262–269	Problem Solving	153–157		•	•	•		•		•		•		•	•	•			•	
	3	270–277	Multiplication	158–162				•		•	•	•		•	•	•		•			•	
	4	278–285	Division	163–167			•	•	•	•	•	•		•		•		•			•	
	5	286–293	Fractions	168–172		•	•	•		•		•		•		•	•	•			•	
Unit 9 Shaping Questions	1	302–309	Solid Shapes	174–180		•	•	•	•	•		•	•	•	•	•		•			•	
	2	310–317	Geometric Questions	181–185		•	•	•		•	•	•		•		•		•	•		•	
	3	318–325	Shape Riddles	186–190		•	•	•		•		•		•	•	•		•			•	
Unit 10 Anything's Possible	1	334–341	Collecting Data	192–198	•	•	•	•	•	•	•		•	•		•		•	•		•	
	2	342–349	Making Predictions	199–205		•	•	•	•	•		•		•		•		•			•	
The Parade				206–215		•	•	•		•		•		•	•	•		•			•	•
A Trip to the Nature Center				216–225		•	•	•	•	•	•	•	•	•	•	•		•		•	•	•

How is *Skill Power* organized?

There are 225 pages in the second-grade *Skill Power book*—approximately six pages to use with each week of the *MathLand* program. *Skill Power* is a collection of different types of pages that rotate sequentially throughout the book and are designed to provide balanced, ongoing practice in problem solving, computation skills, and mathematical concepts.

Included on many pages are Assessment Tips that give you ideas for using the problems as assessment tools, hints about what to look for in children's work, or ways to extend the learning. On many student pages are Parent Notes that explain the "why" of specific problems, the philosophy behind the *MathLand* approach to mathematics, and ideas for integrating math into everyday life.

The following chart shows the sequence of page types for each week of a *MathLand* unit.

MathLand Unit Weeks	Vocabulary	Mixed Skills Practice	Unit Correlation Problems	Special Focus
First week	2 pages	3 pages	1 page	1 to 2 pages
Following weeks		3 pages	1 page	1 to 2 pages

The problems in *Skill Power* invite a diversity of problem-solving strategies. Although the problems may be more challenging for children than those presented orally in class in *Daily Tune-Ups*, children can find solutions by using their developing mathematical understandings and their own reasoning skills. Encouraging children to find and use different solution strategies for the same problem will enhance children's thinking abilities and sharpen their computation skills.

On pages T6 to T8 you will find three letters—one to the student, one to the family, and one to the student and family—that will help you communicate with students and families about the types of problems they will be seeing in *Skill Power*. You can choose to send all three letters home at the beginning of the school year, or you may wish to send them home over a period of time.

What is *Skill Power*?

Skill Power is a collection of problems designed to increase children's computation and problem-solving skills through daily practice in a thinking environment. Like *Daily Tune-Ups*, *Skill Power* makes use of short, frequent, repetitive math problems so children build fluency in a variety of math concepts. Perfect for homework or for in-class written assignments, *Skill Power* is challenging, fun, and promotes smart thinking!

How do I use *Skill Power*?

There are different options for integrating *Skill Power* into your mathematics program. If you have *MathLand*, you can start *Skill Power* along with the first unit of *MathLand* and use it consecutively throughout the school year. Or, you can refer to the guidebook correlation (pages iv-v) to select those pages that best fit the particular needs of your children. These problems can also be used to supplement and enhance other mathematics programs.

We recommend working through several samples of each type of problem together with the class, explaining that for some problems there may be more than one correct answer and that children's solution explanations may vary. Assign the pages as homework or use them in class for individual or group practice. Have children work all the problems on a page, writing explanations for one or two problems, or have them solve selected problems only. For most of their work, children will record their explanations on blank paper.

Allowing time for children to discuss their work in small groups or with the whole class will promote greater understanding and increased communication skills. Encourage children to talk through their problem-solving processes by saying, **Tell me about your thinking. How can you convince me that your answer is correct?** Have children choose examples of "smart arithmetic" for their portfolios. They will be impressed to see their progress over the school year.

One of the frailest of human faculties is the ability to remember isolated bits of information such as "rules" accepted on faith without understanding. The child who is made dependent on his ability to memorize is painfully vulnerable. When he forgets, he is helpless; when he thinks he remembers, he is never sure.

Robert Wirtz
Drill and Practice at the Problem-Solving Level

▼

What work will children do?

The variety and repetition of page types in *Skill Power* give children the opportunity to refine and enhance their conceptual understanding, problem solving, and computation skills as the year progresses. The content of these pages includes: vocabulary, arithmetic computation, story problems, equation formulation, estimation, and test practice. Although most problems have one correct answer, children may surprise you with the variety of solution strategies they develop as their number sense and mathematical thinking skills increase.

Vocabulary

At the beginning of each unit is a selection of terms and definitions for children to use when writing or talking about *MathLand* investigations. Also included is a page that allows children to practice writing the math terms. You may want to include these and other words in a class word bank for each unit. You can also have children compile these pages into their own vocabulary booklets.

Estimation

Estimation is a vital skill for children to develop. It allows them to verify whether an answer is reasonable and leads to greater mental computation ability. Encourage children to use an estimate before, during, and after finding an exact answer whenever appropriate. With practice, children will become increasingly more adept at estimating, often using estimation to reformulate problems—changing them so they're easier to solve using mental computation. You will find many opportunities for using estimation on the mixed-skills practice pages.

Test Practice

At the end of *Skill Power* are two 10-page booklets to use for test practice. Each booklet has one theme for all of the problems. If you choose to have children complete these pages, you may want to do so at different times of the year—before standardized testing and at the end of the year, for example. The intent of these pages is to familiarize children with the conditions of testing: working individually, without assistance, on familiar and unfamiliar problems. (You should read the problems aloud to the class.) Children can attempt the problems on their own, then discuss them as a class. One focus of the discussion should be, **What is the question asking?** Remember to emphasize to children and parents that these booklets are for test practice purposes; they are not actual assessments of children's learning in *MathLand* this year.

What is the "Convince Me!" approach to problem solving?

"Convince Me!" is a unique approach to computational problem solving. Unlike other approaches that depend on children memorizing rote procedures, "Convince Me!" relies on number sense, thinking, and logical discussion to arrive at correct answers to arithmetic problems, and it results in children who are more proficient in computation.

The "Convince Me!" philosophy is based on the belief that children can make their own sense out of number situations and can determine correct answers as they discuss their ideas. You will notice that children who are encouraged to think logically about the numbers in a situation will usually work from left to right, preserving the meaning of the whole numbers. When children are told to follow rote procedures like, "Always start with the ones," before such a rule makes sense to them, they often abandon their own thinking about problems.

Have children use the "Convince Me!" approach for many of the problems in this book. Children should record their solution to a problem, then use words, pictures, and numbers to tell about the thinking that led to the solution. Explain to the children that they want to explain in a way that convinces others their answer makes sense. You will notice that, as children write or tell about their strategies, they often identify and correct errors they have made.

Children who work in the "Convince Me!" way will be able to solve double- and multi-digit addition and subtraction problems using their own reasoning and number understandings. Because the thinking is their own, they will be able to explain their strategies to each other. As children discuss their thinking—challenging, justifying, and verifying their strategies—they learn strategies from each other, adopting new ones as they are ready. In this way, the classroom becomes an algorithm-rich environment.

Computation Problems

Children will use the "Convince Me!" approach to solve most computation problems involving operations of whole numbers, fractions, money, and measurement. Many problems ask children to explain their thinking or to tell how they know the answer is correct. Explanations should include the precise steps children used to calculate answers. This will take practice. When children say, "I just did it in my head," ask them to explain exactly what they did.

> 1. Write the answer. Tell how you know. 15 − 3 = 12
>
> I know that because if you take away three from five you get two so if you take away three from 15 you get 12 because if you take away 1 from 15 you get 14 and if you take away 2 from 15 you get 13 and so if you take away 3 from 15 you get 12.

◀ This child told how he subtracted 3 from 15. He gave a complete, if somewhat wordy, explanation. By seeing an example of his thinking, as well as the actual computation, you get an idea of whether the child understood the problem and whether or not he could do similar computations.

Story Problems

Children will solve a variety of story problems, at times writing their own story problems using given data. Many problems have multiple-step solutions. Explanations of their thinking will give you insights into children's reasoning abilities and problem-analysis skills.

◀ This child restated the problem and then drew a simple picture to show the answer. Although he did not write down how he knew the answer was 4 balls, his drawing left no doubt that he understood what the question was and how he could demonstrate the solution.

The Answer Is...

When children are asked to write a number of equations having the same answer, their facility with and understanding of number relationships becomes evident. Some children will focus on one or two operations, or equations having just two addends, two factors, and so on. Other children may create complex, multi-operation equations. You will learn a great deal about your children's computational skills on these pages. You can challenge children further by stipulating that equations must have three or more addends. Have children put early responses in their portfolios and then, later in the year, present the same The Answer Is... and compare children's growing number sense and facility with operations.

Dear Student,

Skill Power is a collection of challenging arithmetic problems that may be used for class work or homework. There are some special pages that will help you practice and review mental computation ("Convince Me!"), estimation, and test-taking skills.

You'll begin each unit by learning or reviewing a few vocabulary terms and then using the words for a puzzle or an activity. During the year, you'll be solving different types of problems. After solving a problem, you are often asked to "show your thinking." That means you need to explain how you got your answer. Other questions ask how solving one problem can help you solve similar problems. Use a separate piece of paper so you have enough space to draw or write about your thinking. (Sometimes your teacher may ask you to show your thinking for just one problem.)

Usually, there is only one correct answer to a problem, but there may be many different ways to find that answer. Talk with your classmates about how you figured out the answers. You'll learn how to convince them your thinking is correct. Listen to their ideas. You'll probably learn other ways to solve a problem!

If you are using *Skill Power* for homework, share your thinking with your family as you solve the problems. Remember, good thinking takes time!

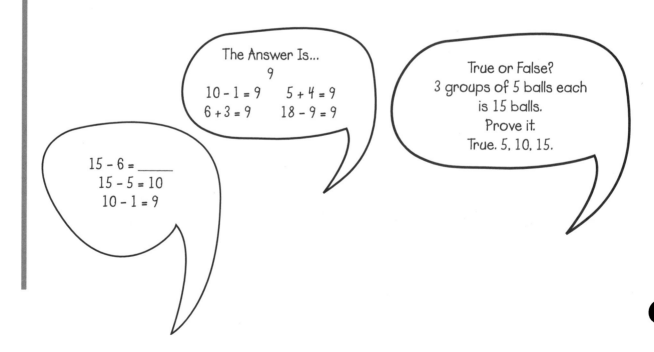

Dear Family,

The arithmetic problems in *Skill Power* focus on building number sense. Children are asked not only to get the correct answers, but also to explain their thinking. This emphasis on reasoning skills gives children a strong arithmetic base. These exercises also include multiple-choice and true/false problems to prepare children for the format and language they might see on tests.

To encourage good thinking, most problems ask the student to prove an answer or tell about his or her reasoning. While there is usually one correct answer to a problem, there may be many different strategies or ways to arrive at that answer. The more strategies children develop, the more efficient and confident they become as problem solvers.

You will probably find it interesting to work with your child as he or she works in *Skill Power*. Express your appreciation for the effort and thinking your child shows and for the explanations he or she writes. If your child makes an error, instead of saying "wrong" or telling the correct answer, help your child to rethink the answer. You could repeat the child's explanation in a questioning tone of voice. Or, comment on the reasonableness of the answer. "Twenty-five seems pretty big to me. I need some more convincing." You want to communicate the message that your child's thinking is important.

Here is a sample of an actual response to a typical problem for the second grade. The emphasis is on having children find correct solution methods that make sense to them, and also on explaining or showing their thinking.

This problem involves division, which most second graders will not know as such. Yet most of them, when given such a problem, will find a way to solve it. This child has shown three different ways to state her answer. Any one way would be acceptable and prove that she understood the question. Rather than writing about her thinking, she made two different diagrams to show how many cookies each child gets. She also included an equation to show that there are 6 fives in 30.

Dear Student and Family,

Children will encounter a variety of mathematical skills and concepts in *Skill Power*: addition, subtraction, multiplication, division, fractions, measurement, and more. There are many mixed-practice pages in *Skill Power,* and once a week, a problem related to the unit topic is presented. In addition, children will find some "special focus" pages in this book:

Race to the Finish pages are one of the many ways children will be building speed with mental arithmetic in their mathematics studies this year. Reliable recall of basic addition and subtraction facts is essential for carrying out computations quickly and accurately.

Follow the Trail pages provide another way for children to visualize and think about double-digit addition and subtraction. The first pages introduce the 100 Number Board and the rules for following the arrow directions. Then children use the board as a "calculating device" to find sums and differences.

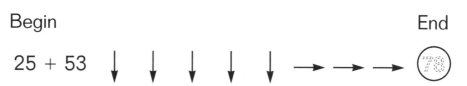

What's My Rule? pages engage children in lots of addition and subtraction as they try to figure out the rule a computer is applying to change the numbers entered into its program.

In	Out
3	6
10	13
5	8
9	12
6	9
1	4

The rule is _____add 3_____ .

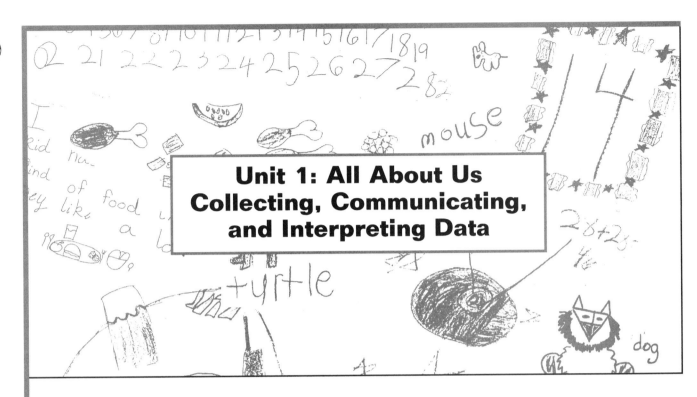

Unit 1: All About Us
Collecting, Communicating, and Interpreting Data

Thinking Questions

What are the favorite lunches and dinners of your classmates? What kinds of pets do you and your classmates have? How many teeth have the children in your class lost?

Investigations

In this MathLand unit, you will organize and record data to help you find answers to these questions and more. You will be making up surveys about things you want to know. You will learn how to use the surveys to gather data.

Real-World Math

Using surveys to collect, organize, and record information is fun and interesting. What information would you like to find out from a survey of your family or friends?

Math Vocabulary

You will be using these new words to talk about collecting and reporting information.

Asking **How many . . . ?** is a good way to get information. In this unit, you ask questions such as How many books do you read in a week? Then you record the information.

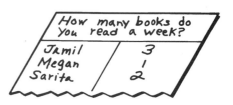

To **organize** things is to arrange them in an order that makes sense.

Example: José organized his shoes in his closet.

To **sort** is to group together things that are alike in some way.

Example: Tanya likes to sort her markers, crayons, and pencils.

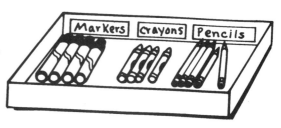

A **survey** is a way to gather information from many people. You ask a question and record the answers you get.

Example: Michiko used a survey to find out about her friends' pets.

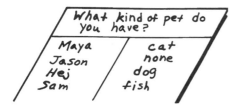

Word Practice

Practice writing the math words on the lines below.

How many . . . ?

_____

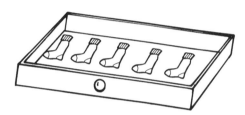

organize

_____

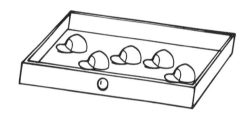

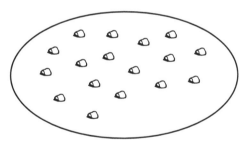

sort

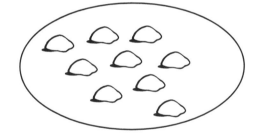

_____

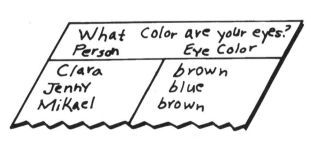

survey

_____

Name _____

1

Write the Answers

2 + 2 = ___

3 + 3 = ___

4 + 4 = ___

5 + 5 = ___

Tell how you know.

2

How Many Cents?

A   1¢

B   4¢

C   5¢

D   3¢

Tell how you know.

3

Agree or Disagree?

2, 4, 6, 8, 10,

The next number is 11.
Do you agree or disagree?

Explain your thinking.

4

Time for Lunch!

There are 2 children eating lunch.
Each has 2 hot dogs.

How many hot dogs are there in all?

Show your thinking.

▼ **PARENT NOTE:**
Once children have found the answer to a problem, they are invited to use any combination of words, pictures, and numbers to explain their thinking about a problem.

1

The Answer Is 8

Write 6 equations that have this answer.

2

Write the Answers

5 + 5 = ___

5 + 4 = ___

4 + 4 = ___

4 + 3 = ___

Tell how you know.

3

What Number Is Missing?

66, 67, 68, ___, 70

A 71   C 69

B 9   D 59

Tell how you know.

4

True or False?

Here are 20 stars.

☆ ☆ ☆ ☆ ☆

☆ ☆ ☆ ☆ ☆

☆ ☆ ☆ ☆ ☆

☆ ☆ ☆ ☆ ☆

Prove it.

▼ **PARENT NOTE:**
The Answer Is... problems ask children to find several ways to represent the same number. For example, the number 24 is 12 + 12, 4 + 4 + 4 + 4 + 4 + 4, half of 48, one less than 25, 20 + 4, and so on.

1

Balloons

You have 25 balloons.
15 blow away.
9 pop.

How many balloons are left?

Write about your thinking.

2

The Answer Is 12

Write at least 4 equations that have this answer.

3

Write the Answer

$$\begin{array}{r} 3 \\ +8 \\ \hline \end{array}$$

Show your thinking.

4

What Is the Next Number?

10, 12, 14, 16, ___

A 18   C 17

B 19   D 15

Tell how you know.

What Time Is It?

Write the missing numbers on the clocks.
Draw hands on each clock. Write the time.

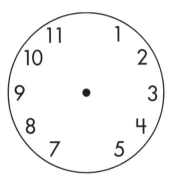

_____

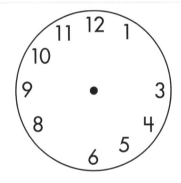

_____

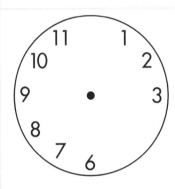

_____

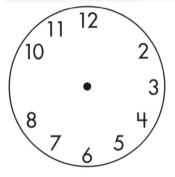

_____

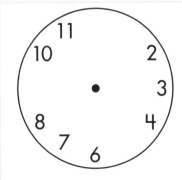

_____

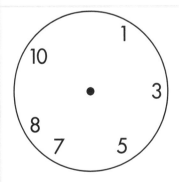

_____

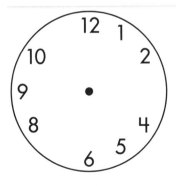

_____

_____

_____

Race to the Finish

How fast can you add and subtract numbers in your head?

Start at the bicycle. Race to the finish line.

Add or subtract the numbers along the way.

Write your subtotals in the squares.

Write your total on the finish line.

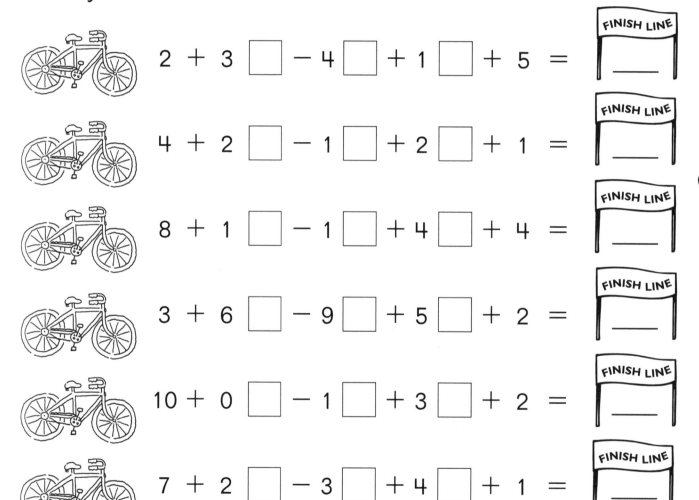

▼ PARENT NOTE:
Arithmetic problems in *Skill Power* are designed to help children develop strong mental computation skills and the ability to handle numbers in many ways.

Name _____

True or False?

This is 11¢.

Prove it.

Pets

There are 20 children in a class.
10 have 1 pet.
10 have 2 pets.

How many pets are there in all?

Show your thinking.

The Answer Is 9

Write 5 equations that have this answer.

Write the Answer

12 + 6 = ___

Tell how you know.

PARENT NOTE:
On pages like this, children are given a variety of different problems. Deciding how to approach each one adds challenge and builds mathematical reasoning skills.

1

Which Equals 5?

○ 10 − 5

○ 8 − 2

○ 7 + 2

○ 4 + 2

Tell how you know.

2

True or False?

The clock says 12 o'clock.

Tell how you know.

3

Bug Eyes

There are 19 bugs.
Each has 2 big eyes.

How many bug eyes are there in all?

Show your thinking.

4

The Answer Is 14

Write 6 equations that have this answer.

1 Write the Answer

$15 - 3 =$ ___

Use pictures, words, or numbers to explain your thinking.

2 Which Coin Is 10¢?

A   C

B   D

Tell how you know.

3 True or False?

3 groups of 5 balls each is 15 balls.

Prove it.

4 How Much Fruit?

Marla has 3 apples. She has 4 bananas and 6 plums.

How many does she have in all?

Show your thinking.

What Pets Do You Have?

The children in Mr. Vinh's class made this chart.
What can you say about the chart?
Write as many things as you can.

What pets do you have?			
Dog	Cat	Bird	Fish

Race to the Finish

How fast can you add and subtract numbers in your head?
Start at the bicycle. Race to the finish line.
Add or subtract the numbers along the way.
Write your subtotals in the squares.
Write your total on the finish line.

 16 + 2 ☐ − 4 ☐ + 3 ☐ + 1 =
_____

13 + 1 ☐ − 5 ☐ + 2 ☐ + 4 =
_____

 20 − 6 ☐ − 4 ☐ + 2 ☐ − 5 =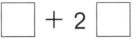
_____

17 + 0 ☐ − 1 ☐ − 2 ☐ + 3 =
_____

 18 − 9 ☐ + 3 ☐ + 4 ☐ + 2 =
_____

 14 + 2 ☐ − 2 ☐ − 7 ☐ + 1 =
_____

Race to the Finish

How fast can you add and subtract numbers in your head?

Start at the bicycle. Race to the finish line.

Add or subtract the numbers along the way.

Write your subtotals in the squares.

Write your total on the finish line.

$9 + 4\ \square + 1\ \square + 6\ \square - 7\ =$ FINISH LINE ____

$8 + 5\ \square + 2\ \square + 5\ \square - 8\ =$ FINISH LINE ____

$7 + 6\ \square + 3\ \square + 4\ \square - 5\ =$ FINISH LINE ____

$6 + 4\ \square + 3\ \square - 10\ \square + 3\ =$ FINISH LINE ____

$5 + 5\ \square - 5\ \square + 5\ \square - 5\ =$ FINISH LINE ____

$3 + 5\ \square + 2\ \square + 0\ \square - 10\ =$ FINISH LINE ____

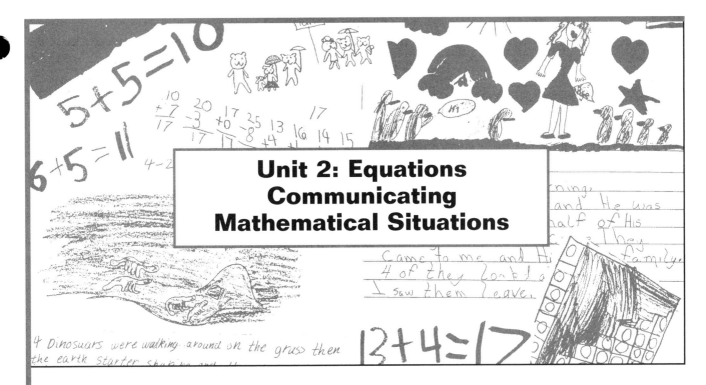

Thinking Questions

How do you show addition and subtraction stories with equations? How can you use grids to show equations? What kinds of patterns are in equation grids? How many equations are there for each number?

Investigations

You and your classmates will explore ways of recording equations in this MathLand unit. You will also be writing and illustrating addition and subtraction stories that match equations for a class math magazine.

Real-World Math

Matching number stories and equations can be an enjoyable family activity. You can play games and learn addition and subtraction facts at the same time.

Math Vocabulary

You will be using these new words to talk about adding and subtracting numbers.

A **pattern** is an order of a set of things that repeats. Numbers, shapes, and colors are some things that can follow a pattern.

An **addition equation** tells about putting numbers together. It has numbers, an addition sign, and an equal sign. It has equal values on both sides of the equal sign.

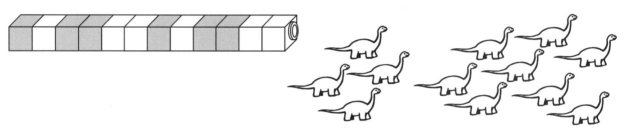

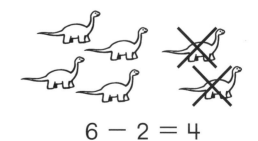

$$4 + 8 = 12$$

To be **equal** is to have the same value. We use an **equal sign** in equations.

Example: 9 is equal to 6 + 3. We write 9 = 6 + 3.

A **subtraction equation** tells about taking away one number from another.

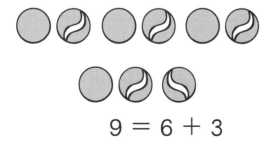

$$9 = 6 + 3$$

$$6 - 2 = 4$$

Word Practice

Practice writing the math words on the lines below.

 =

equal

_____

$15 + 4 = 19$ $11 + 3 = 14$

addition

_____

$13 - 7 = 6$ $20 - 20 = 0$

subtraction

_____

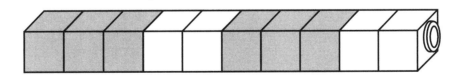

pattern

_____

1

The Answer Is 15

Write at least 5 equations that have this answer.

2

Write the Answer

How many dots are here?

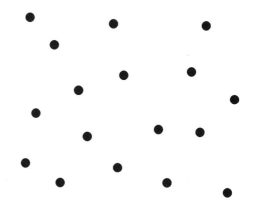

Explain how you know.

3

Choose the Answer

12 − 7 = ___

A 6

B 8

C 15

D 5

Tell how you know.

4

True or False?

This is 10¢.

Prove it.

1

At the Pool

Carlos swam 3 laps at the pool 3 times.
Aaron swam 4 laps at the pool 4 times.

How many laps did the boys swim in all?

Show your thinking.

The Answer Is 16

Write 2 addition equations and 2 subtraction equations that have this answer.

3

Write the Answers

$$\begin{array}{r} 5 \\ +5 \\ \hline \end{array} \qquad \begin{array}{r} 6 \\ +6 \\ \hline \end{array} \qquad \begin{array}{r} 7 \\ +7 \\ \hline \end{array}$$

Tell how you know.

Choose the Answer

Marla had 25¢. She spent 15¢. How much did she have left?

○ 10¢   ○ 15¢

○ 5¢   ○ 20¢

Tell how you know.

▼ **PARENT NOTE:**
Thinking about a related problem in order to solve a computation is a powerful skill. In problem 3 for example, your child may use the knowledge that 5 and 5 is 10 to solve for 6 and 6.

▼1 True or False?

6 is an even number.

Prove it.

▼2 How Much?

José has

How much does he have in all?
Can he buy a ball for 15¢?

Show your thinking.

▼3 The Answer Is 20

Write 7 equations that have this answer.

▼4 Write the Answers

10 + 7 = ___

10 + 3 = ___

10 + 9 = ___

Tell how you know.

▼ **PARENT NOTE:**
Children who learn to make sense of arithmetic start their study of mathematics on a strong footing. In *Skill Power*, your child is asked to use logical thinking and everything he or she knows about numbers to solve problems.

What Time Is It?

Write the times the clocks show.

3:00
_____

3 o'clock
_____

_____

_____

2:30
_____

two thirty
_____

_____

_____

_____

_____

_____

_____

Race to the Finish

How fast can you add and subtract numbers in your head?

Start at the bicycle. Race to the finish line.

Add or subtract the numbers along the way.

Write your subtotals in the squares.

Write your total on the finish line.

 $2 - 1\ \square + 3\ \square + 6\ \square + 0 = $ FINISH LINE ____

 $3 + 4\ \square + 2\ \square - 9\ \square - 0 = $ FINISH LINE ____

 $5 - 3\ \square + 5\ \square - 0\ \square + 3 = $ FINISH LINE ____

 $5 + 3\ \square - 0\ \square + 7\ \square + 1 = $ FINISH LINE ____

 $9 + 4\ \square + 1\ \square + 4\ \square - 0 = $ FINISH LINE ____

 $2 + 2\ \square + 3\ \square - 0\ \square + 7 = $ FINISH LINE ____

1

What Time Is It?

_____

Tell how you know.

2

Agree or Disagree?

4, 14, 24, 34, 44, ___

The next number is 55.
Do you agree or disagree?

Show your thinking.

3

Write the Answers

10 is ____ more than 5.

12 is ____ more than 6.

14 is ____ more than 7.

16 is ____ more than 8.

Show your thinking.

4

Write the Answer

11 − 3 = ___

Use these dots to help you.

Tell how you know.

1
Write the Answers

13 − 3 = ___

15 − 5 = ___

17 − 7 = ___

Tell how you know.

2
How Many Bones?

2 dogs have 4 bones.
They share them equally.

How many bones will each dog get?

A 4   C 1

B 2   D 3

Explain how you know.

3
True or False?

You can make a true equation with 7, 13, 6.

Prove it.

4
Ducks in a Puddle

There are 5 ducks playing in a puddle.
Soon 9 more ducks come to play.
Then 5 more ducks come.

How many ducks are there in all?

Explain your thinking.

PARENT NOTE:

Mental computation is a challenging activity that builds reasoning skills and number understandings. Children are challenged to solve as many problems in *Skill Power* as they can mentally.

1

The Answer Is 15¢

Draw coins to show
3 different ways to
make 15¢.

 2

Write the Answers

4 + 5 = ___

5 + 6 = ___

6 + 7 = ___

7 + 8 = ___

Tell how you know.

 3

Horses in Pens

There are 16 horses and
4 pens. The same number
of horses go in each pen.

How many horses are in
each pen?

○ 5   ○ 4

○ 6   ○ 3

Show your thinking.

 4

True or False?

The clock says 11:30.

Tell how you know.

Write More Equations

Write more equations in the boxes.
Make them all different.

4	5	6	7
		2 + 2 + 2 = 6	
	5 + 0 = 5		6 + 1 = 7
1 + 1 + 1 + 1 = 4		3 + 3 = 6	
2 + 2 = 4			

Race to the Finish

How fast can you add and subtract numbers in your head?

Start at the bicycle. Race to the finish line.

Add or subtract the numbers along the way.

Write your subtotals in the squares.

Write your total on the finish line.

 5 + 4 ☐ − 3 ☐ − 2 ☐ + 1 = | FINISH LINE _____

 20 − 1 ☐ − 2 ☐ − 3 ☐ − 4 = | FINISH LINE _____

 6 + 5 ☐ + 4 ☐ + 3 ☐ + 2 = | FINISH LINE _____

 20 − 2 ☐ − 3 ☐ − 4 ☐ − 5 = | FINISH LINE _____

 4 + 3 ☐ + 2 ☐ + 1 ☐ − 0 = | FINISH LINE _____

20 − 3 ☐ − 4 ☐ − 5 ☐ − 6 = | FINISH LINE _____

1

Frogs in Puddles

There are 6 frogs and
2 puddles.
There is the same number
of frogs in each puddle.

How many frogs are in
each puddle?

Write about your thinking.

2

The Answer Is 10¢

Draw coins to show
2 different ways to
make 10¢.

Do not use any dimes.

3

Write the Answers

$$\begin{array}{r} 9 \\ -7 \\ \hline \end{array} \qquad \begin{array}{r} 7 \\ -5 \\ \hline \end{array} \qquad \begin{array}{r} 5 \\ -3 \\ \hline \end{array}$$

Tell how you know.

4

Choose the Answer

3 tens is the same as ____ .

A   100 ones

B   10 ones

C   300 ones

D   30 ones

Tell how you know.

1 ▽ True or False?

There are 3 more triangles than squares.

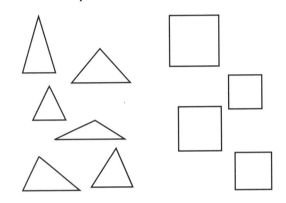

Prove it.

2 ▽ How Many Sheep?

There were 14 sheep in the field.
9 jumped over the fence.

How many sheep were left?

Show your thinking.

3 ▽ The Answer Is 24

Write 6 equations that have this answer.

4 ▽ Write the Answers

10 + 2 = ___

9 + 2 = ___

10 + 4 = ___

9 + 4 = ___

Tell how you know.

1

Choose the Answer

Which is the same as
4 + 4?

○ 5 + 4

○ 6 + 3

○ 2 + 6

○ 8 + 1

Tell how you know.

2

True or False?

10 − 6 has the same
answer as 9 − 5.

Prove it.

3

How Many Wheels?

There are 3 bikes in front
of the school.
There are 2 wheels on
each bike.

How many wheels are
there in all?

Show your thinking.

4

The Answer Is 20¢

Draw coins to show
4 different ways to
make 20¢.

100 Number Board

1	2	3	4	5	6	7	8	9	10
11	12	13	14	15	16	17	18	19	20
21	22	23	24	25	26	27	28	29	30
31	32	33	34	35	36	37	38	39	40
41	42	43	44	45	46	47	48	49	50
51	52	53	54	55	56	57	58	59	60
61	62	63	64	65	66	67	68	69	70
71	72	73	74	75	76	77	78	79	80
81	82	83	84	85	86	87	88	89	90
91	92	93	94	95	96	97	98	99	100

1. Count by twos up to 30. Color those numbers red.
2. Find the odd numbers from 1 to 29.
   Color them green.
3. Count by tens. Color those numbers blue.
4. Find all the numbers that start with 7.
   Color them yellow.
5. Find the last 4 numbers. Color them brown.

Race to the Finish

How fast can you add and subtract numbers in your head?

Start at the bicycle. Race to the finish line.

Add or subtract the numbers along the way.

Write your subtotals in the squares.

Write your total on the finish line.

 $1 + 2\ \square + 3\ \square + 4\ \square - 4 =$ FINISH LINE _____

 $2 + 3\ \square + 4\ \square + 5\ \square - 5 =$ FINISH LINE _____

 $3 + 4\ \square + 5\ \square + 6\ \square - 6 =$ FINISH LINE _____

 $4 + 5\ \square + 6\ \square + 7\ \square - 7 =$ FINISH LINE _____

 $6 + 5\ \square + 4\ \square + 3\ \square - 3 =$ FINISH LINE _____

 $5 + 4\ \square + 3\ \square + 2\ \square - 2 =$ FINISH LINE _____

1   Write the Answers

10	9	8
+10	+9	+8

Tell how you know.

2   Choose the Answer

Which number comes just before 40?

A   39

B   38

C   41

D   29

Show your thinking.

3   True or False?

11 is 4 more than 7.

Prove it.

4   How Many Pennies?

You have 9 pennies.
You give 3 away.
You lose 2.

How many pennies do you have left?

Show your thinking.

1 ▼

The Answer Is 25¢

Draw coins to show
4 different ways to
make 25¢.

2 ▼

Write the Answer

$$7 + 7 = \underline{}$$

Tell about your thinking.

3 ▼

Which Makes 19?

A   10 + 10

B   9 + 10

C   9 + 11

D   8 + 12

Tell how you know.

4 ▼

Agree or Disagree?

27 is the next number
after 25. Do you agree
or disagree?

Show your thinking.

How Many Hours?

Tran worked after school.
He worked 7 hours in
one week.
Then he worked 11 hours,
3 hours, and 5 hours.

How many hours did he
work in all?

Show your thinking.

Greater Than 9

Write 3 numbers that are
greater than 9.

Explain your thinking.

Write the Answers

12	14	16
−6	−7	−8

Tell how you know.

Choose the Answer

18 − 7 = ___

A 13

B 12

C 11

D 10

Explain how you know.

The Answer Is 10

Write 10 different equations that have this answer.
Write both addition and subtraction equations.

Race to the Finish

How fast can you add and subtract numbers in your head?

Start at the bicycle. Race to the finish line.

Add or subtract the numbers along the way.

Write your subtotals in the squares.

Write your total on the finish line.

 $18 - 3 \ \square - 3 \ \square - 3 \ \square - 3 =$ FINISH LINE ____

 $12 + 2 \ \square + 2 \ \square + 2 \ \square + 2 =$ FINISH LINE ____

 $14 + 1 \ \square + 1 \ \square + 1 \ \square + 1 =$ FINISH LINE ____

 $19 - 4 \ \square - 4 \ \square - 4 \ \square - 4 =$ FINISH LINE ____

 $17 - 2 \ \square - 2 \ \square - 2 \ \square - 2 =$ FINISH LINE ____

 $20 - 5 \ \square - 5 \ \square - 5 \ \square - 5 =$ FINISH LINE ____

1

True or False?

One half of 6 is 3.

Prove it.

2

How Many Legs?

There are 3 cows.
Each cow has 4 legs.

How many legs are there in all?

Show your thinking.

3

The Answer Is 21

Write 3 addition equations and 3 subtraction equations that have this answer.

4

Write the Answer

$$\begin{array}{r} 12 \\ + 8 \\ \hline \end{array}$$

Tell how you know.

1

Choose the Answer

There are 2 tricycles.
Each tricycle has 3 wheels.

How many wheels are there in all?

A 9   C 6

B 4   D 8

Tell how you know.

2

Agree or Disagree?

83 comes between 82 and 84. Do you agree or disagree?

Show your thinking.

3

How Many Books?

There are 12 books on Alicia's desk.
There are 24 books on the table.

How many books are there in all?

Show your thinking.

4

The Answer Is 17

Write at least 5 equations that have this answer.

① Write the Answers

$$8 \atop +7$$ $$8 \atop +8$$ $$8 \atop +9$$

Tell how you know.

② Choose the Answer

What is 25 + 25 between?

○ 45 and 60

○ 30 and 40

○ 25 and 30

○ 55 and 60

Explain how you know.

③ True or False?

9 is an even number.

Prove it.

④ How Many Toys?

There were 16 toys on the floor.
Jon put 8 toys away.
Tomas got out 6 more toys.

How many toys are there now?

Show your thinking.

Keeping Track

Fill in this chart.

   _____3_____

   _____

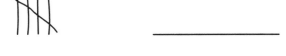   _____

   _____

   _____

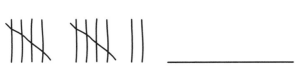   _____

Write your own tally.   How many is it?

_____   _____

Race to the Finish

How fast can you add and subtract numbers in your head?

Start at the bicycle. Race to the finish line.

Add or subtract the numbers along the way.

Write your subtotals in the squares.

Write your total on the finish line.

 $2 + 3 \boxed{} - 1 \boxed{} + 3 \boxed{} + 3 =$ **FINISH LINE** ____

 $4 + 4 \boxed{} + 5 \boxed{} + 5 \boxed{} - 1 =$ **FINISH LINE** ____

 $6 + 3 \boxed{} - 1 \boxed{} + 3 \boxed{} + 6 =$ **FINISH LINE** ____

 $7 - 1 \boxed{} + 2 \boxed{} + 7 \boxed{} + 2 =$ **FINISH LINE** ____

 $1 + 1 \boxed{} - 1 \boxed{} + 9 \boxed{} + 9 =$ **FINISH LINE** ____

$8 + 1 \boxed{} - 1 \boxed{} + 8 \boxed{} + 1 =$ **FINISH LINE** ____

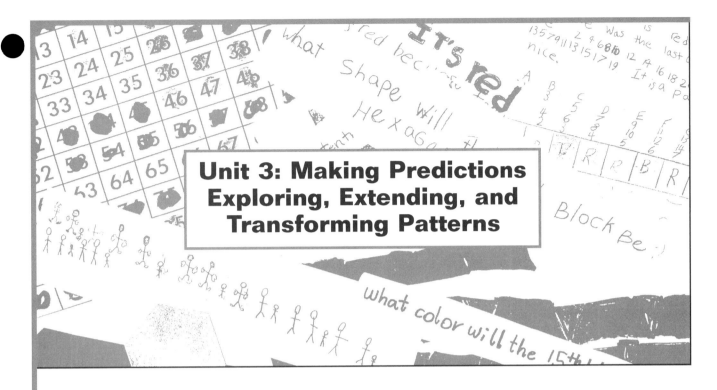

**Unit 3: Making Predictions
Exploring, Extending, and
Transforming Patterns**

Thinking Questions

If a pattern is twenty tiles long, how can you find out
what color the tenth tile will be? How many blocks will
it take to build a wall with three towers? How can you
use your pattern to predict what will come next?

Investigations

You will learn about patterns in this MathLand unit.
You will learn how to use prediction and counting to
find ways of answering your questions about patterns.

Real-World Math

There are many different patterns in the world. Look for
patterns on city streets, buildings, floors, and counter
tops. What do you think the person who made the
design had to know to make that pattern?

Math Vocabulary

You will be using these new words to talk about patterns.

To **predict** is to tell what you think will happen.

Example: I predict that the next circle will be gray.

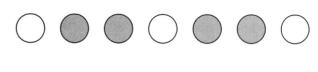

A **pattern** is an order of a set of things that repeats. Numbers, shapes, and colors are some things that can follow a pattern. Once you figure out a pattern, you can predict what comes next.

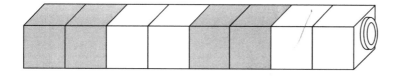

Grid paper is a tool for recording some kinds of information.
It helps you record LinkerCube trains.

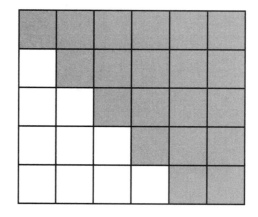

Word Practice

Practice writing the math words on the lines below.

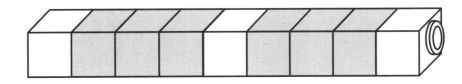

pattern   _____

predict   _____

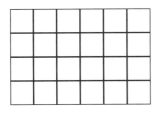   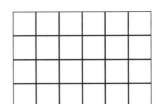

grid paper   _____

1

The Answer Is 31

Write 7 equations that have this answer.

2

Write the Answers

$$13 \quad 13 \quad 13$$
$$-3 \quad -4 \quad -5$$

Tell how you know.

3

Choose the Answer

What is the next number?

4, 8, 12, 16, ___

A 19   C 21

B 20   D 22

Tell about your thinking.

4

True or False?

$$15 + 6 = 21$$

Prove it.

PARENT NOTE:
There are usually several correct ways children can arrive at the answers for problems in *Skill Power*. As children become aware of this, their willingness to try unfamiliar problems grows.

1 Pizza Time

There are 10 slices of pizza.

How many children could have 2 slices each?

Explain your thinking.

2 Write the Next 3 Numbers

5, 10, 15, ___ ,

___ , ___

Tell how you know.

3 Write the Answers

11 + 9 = ___

12 + 8 = ___

13 + 7 = ___

Tell about your thinking.

4 Choose the Answer

Which number comes just after 62?

A 61

B 66

C 64

D 63

Tell how you know.

1

True or False?

There is 12¢ inside the square.

Prove it.

2

Birds in the Tree

There are 18 birds in the tree.
Each bird has 2 wings.

How many wings are there in all?

Show your thinking.

3

The Answer Is 35

Write 8 equations that have this answer.

4

Write the Answers

5 + 5 = _____

4 + 6 = _____

7 + 7 = _____

6 + 8 = _____

Use words, pictures, or numbers to explain your thinking.

100 Number Board

1	2	3	4	5	6	7	8	9	10
11	12	13	14	15	16	17	18	19	20
21	22	23	24	25	26	27	28	29	30
31	32	33	34	35	36	37	38	39	40
41	42	43	44	45	46	47	48	49	50
51	52	53	54	55	56	57	58	59	60
61	62	63	64	65	66	67	68	69	70
71	72	73	74	75	76	77	78	79	80
81	82	83	84	85	86	87	88	89	90
91	92	93	94	95	96	97	98	99	100

1. Count by threes. Color those numbers red.
2. Count by fives. Color those numbers green.
3. Count by tens. Color those numbers yellow.
4. Count by fours. Color those numbers blue.
5. What numbers did you color more than once?

Name _____

Race to the Finish

How fast can you add and subtract numbers in your head?

Start at the bicycle. Race to the finish line.

Add or subtract the numbers along the way.

Write your subtotals in the squares.

Write your total on the finish line.

 $20 - 3 \;\square\; - 4 \;\square\; + 2 \;\square\; + 4 \;=\;$ **FINISH LINE** ____

 $15 - 5 \;\square\; - 3 \;\square\; + 5 \;\square\; + 4 \;=\;$ **FINISH LINE** ____

 $13 - 6 \;\square\; - 1 \;\square\; + 6 \;\square\; + 2 \;=\;$ **FINISH LINE** ____

 $9 - 2 \;\square\; - 3 \;\square\; + 3 \;\square\; + 1 \;=\;$ **FINISH LINE** ____

 $11 + 2 \;\square\; + 4 \;\square\; - 3 \;\square\; - 1 \;=\;$ **FINISH LINE** ____

 $17 - 2 \;\square\; + 1 \;\square\; - 3 \;\square\; - 1 \;=\;$ **FINISH LINE** ____

Name _____

1 Choose the Answer

19
− 7
———

A 26   C 8

B 13   D 12

Explain how you know.

2 True or False?

One-half hour after
9 o'clock is 10 o'clock.

Prove it.

3 Wagon Wheels

There are 5 wagons
in a row.
Each wagon has 4 wheels.

How many wheels are
there in all?

Write about your thinking.

4 The Answer Is 13

Write 4 addition and
4 subtraction equations
that have this answer.

1

Write the Answers

$6 + 6 = 7 + \bigcirc$

$9 + 9 = 10 + \bigcirc$

$7 + 7 = 8 + \bigcirc$

Tell how you know.

2

What Number Comes Next?

99, 97, 95, 93, ____

○ 91   ○ 92

○ 90   ○ 94

Tell about your thinking.

3

True or False?

21 is greater than 12.

Prove it.

4

Apple Trees

There are 4 trees in the garden.
Each tree has 12 apples on it.

How many apples are there in all?

Show your thinking.

1

The Answer Is 16¢

Draw coins to show 3 different ways to make 16¢.

2

Write the Answers

$5 + 8 = 5 + 5 + \bigcirc$

$8 + 7 = 8 + 2 + \bigcirc$

$7 + 6 = 7 + 3 + \bigcirc$

Tell how you know.

3

Choose the Answer

Which number comes just before 47?

○ 48   ○ 49

○ 45   ○ 46

Tell about your thinking.

4

True or False?

$9 + 8 + 9 = 29$

Prove it.

Calendar Trivia

March

Sun.	Mon.	Tues.	Wed.	Thurs.	Fri.	Sat.
			1	2	3	4
5	6	7	8	9	10	11
12	13	14	15	16	17	18
19	20	21	22	23	24	25
26	27	28	29	30	31	

1. How many numbers have a 1 in them? _____

2. How many even numbers are there? _____

3. How many odd numbers are there? _____

4. How many numbers are there in all? _____

5. Starting with 7, put an X on every 7th number.
What can you say about the numbers with an X on them?

Name _____

Race to the Finish

How fast can you add and subtract numbers in your head?

Start at the bicycle. Race to the finish line.

Add or subtract the numbers along the way.

Write your subtotals in the squares.

Write your total on the finish line.

 $2 + 2 \;\square\; + 1 \;\square\; - 4 \;\square\; + 8 \;=$ FINISH LINE ____

 $3 + 3 \;\square\; - 4 \;\square\; + 1 \;\square\; + 11 \;=$ FINISH LINE ____

 $4 + 4 \;\square\; + 1 \;\square\; + 9 \;\square\; - 3 \;=$ FINISH LINE ____

 $5 + 1 \;\square\; + 2 \;\square\; + 3 \;\square\; - 6 \;=$ FINISH LINE ____

 $4 + 2 \;\square\; + 1 \;\square\; - 7 \;\square\; + 5 \;=$ FINISH LINE ____

 $10 - 3 \;\square\; + 1 \;\square\; + 2 \;\square\; + 6 \;=$ FINISH LINE ____

Race to the Finish

How fast can you add and subtract numbers in your head?
Start at the bicycle. Race to the finish line.
Add or subtract the numbers along the way.
Write your subtotals in the squares.
Write your total on the finish line.

 $14 + 2\ \square + 1\ \square - 5\ \square + 6\ = $ **FINISH LINE** _____

 $9 - 3\ \square + 6\ \square + 4\ \square - 5\ = $ **FINISH LINE** _____

 $7 + 5\ \square + 4\ \square - 1\ \square - 8\ = $ **FINISH LINE** _____

 $18 + 2\ \square - 12\ \square - 3\ \square + 5\ = $ **FINISH LINE** _____

 $20 - 9\ \square + 2\ \square + 3\ \square - 0\ = $ **FINISH LINE** _____

$6 - 2\ \square + 8\ \square + 4\ \square - 3\ = $ **FINISH LINE** _____

Thinking Questions

How do you figure out an equation? What are true equations for a number? How do you know whether an equation is true or false?

Investigations

In this MathLand unit, you will look for number patterns and think about ways equations relate to each other as you and your classmates fill in the Great Addition Chart. You will also discover fact friends that will help you remember equations as you practice.

Real-World Math

There are many ways to find the answers to equations. Think of some different ways of remembering. What ways can you find to share the thinking you used to get your answer?

Math Vocabulary

You will be using these new words to talk about organizing information and explaining thinking.

A **chart** is a tool for organizing information. A chart has rows and columns.
Addition facts can be organized in a chart.

column

+	0	1	2	3	4	5	6
0	0 + 0 = 0	0 + 1 = 0	0 + 2 = 2	0 + 3 = 3	0 + 4 = 4	0 + 5 = 5	0 + 6 = 6
1	1 + 0 = 1	1 + 1 = 2	1 + 2 = 3	1 + 3 = 4	1 + 4 = 5	1 + 5 = 6	1 + 6 = 7
2	2 + 0 = 2	2 + 1 = 3	2 + 2 = 4	2 + 3 = 5	2 + 4 = 6	2 + 5 = 7	2 + 6 =
3		3 + 1 = 3			6	3 + 4 = 7	3 + 5 = 8	3 + 6 =

row

0	0 + 0 = 0	0 + 1 = 0	0 + 2
1	1 + 0 = 1	1 + 1 = 2	1 + 2
2	2 + 0 = 2	2 + 1 = 3	2 + 2

row

A **row** is a horizontal line of spaces in a chart.
Rows go from left to right. The rows are labeled along the left side of a chart.

A **column** is a vertical line of spaces in a chart. Columns go from top to bottom. The columns are labeled along the top of the chart.

column

+	0	1	2	3	
0	0 + 0 = 0	0 + 1 = 0	0 + 2 = 2	0 + 3 = 3	0
1	1 + 0 = 1	1 + 1 = 2	1 + 2 = 3	1 + 3 = 4	1

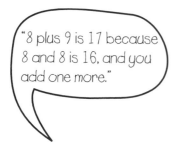

"8 plus 9 is 17 because 8 and 8 is 16, and you add one more."

"That makes sense to me."

To **convince** someone is to explain your thinking so they agree your way of getting an answer really works.

Word Practice

Practice writing the math words on the lines below.

column

5+6=11		5+8=13	5+9=14
6+6=12	6+7=13		6+9=15
	7+7=14	7+8=15	
8+6=14		8+8=16	8+9=17
	9+7=16	9+8=17	9+9=18

row

chart _____

row _____

column _____

"9 + 3. I thought about 10 and 3 is 13, and this is one less. It's 12."

"I get it. So, 9 + 4 would be 13."

convince _____

1

How Much Money?

Antonia counted her money. She said she had 8 take away 5 pennies.

Chris counted his money. He had 9 take away 6 pennies.

Who had more pennies?

Show your thinking.

2

The Answer Is 35¢

Draw coins to show 5 different ways to make 35¢.

3

Write the Answer

10 + 15 = ___

Tell how you know.

4

Choose the Answer

Which clock shows half past 6?

A    C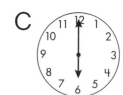

B 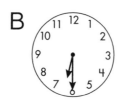   D

Name _____

1

True or False?

Half of 8 is 2.

Prove it.

2

How Many Legs?

Kalil has 2 dogs.
Amy has 2 cats.
Juanita has 3 birds.

How many animal legs are there in all?

Show your thinking.

3

The Answer Is 33

Write 6 equations that have this answer.

4

Write the Answers

$12 + 6 = 10 + \bigcirc$

$15 + 3 = 10 + \bigcirc$

$18 + 1 = 10 + \bigcirc$

Tell how you know.

1 Which Makes 38¢?

A   2 dimes and 2 nickels

B   3 dimes and 3 pennies

C   3 dimes, 1 nickel, and 3 pennies

D   2 dimes, 2 nickels, and 3 pennies

Tell how you know.

2 True or False?

58, 57, 56, 55, ___

The next number is 53.

Prove it.

3 Buzzing Bees

There are 4 bees buzzing on the flower.
Each bee has 6 legs.

How many legs are there in all?

Show your thinking.

4 Making 25¢

Draw 7 coins that together make 25¢.

Name _____

Sharing

1. Show how you would cut the sandwich so you and a friend would each have the same amount.

2. Show how you would cut the pizza so 4 people would each have the same amount.

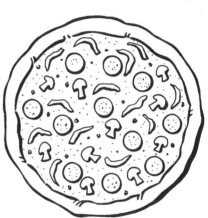

3. Show how you would cut the pie so 8 people would each have the same amount.

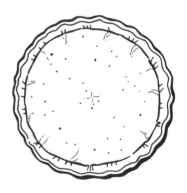

4. Show how you would share the cookies with 3 other children. Give each child the same number.

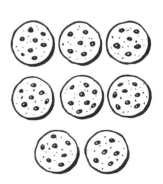

Race to the Finish

How fast can you add and subtract numbers in your head?
Start at the bicycle. Race to the finish line.
Add or subtract the numbers along the way.
Write your subtotals in the squares.
Write your total on the finish line.

$20 - 9 \ \square + 3 \ \square + 3 \ \square + 3 =$ FINISH LINE ____

$13 - 6 \ \square + 7 \ \square + 2 \ \square + 4 =$ FINISH LINE ____

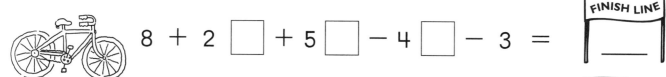
$8 + 2 \ \square + 5 \ \square - 4 \ \square - 3 =$ FINISH LINE ____

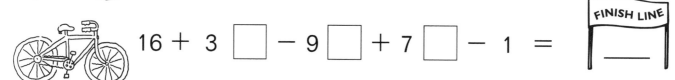
$16 + 3 \ \square - 9 \ \square + 7 \ \square - 1 =$ FINISH LINE ____

$12 + 6 \ \square + 2 \ \square - 10 \ \square + 2 =$ FINISH LINE ____

$17 - 3 \ \square - 3 \ \square + 5 \ \square + 1 =$ FINISH LINE ____

1 Write the Answers

$$
\begin{array}{ccc}
13 & 15 & 17 \\
-4 & -6 & -8 \\
\hline
\end{array}
$$

Tell how you know.

2 What Comes Next?

10¢, 20¢, 30¢, 40¢, ___

A 45¢   C 41¢

B 55¢   D 50¢

Explain your thinking.

3 True or False?

88 is less than 79.

Prove it.

4 Mistress Mary

Mistress Mary planted
1 row of 6 big seeds.
She planted 1 row of
6 little seeds.
Then she planted 1 row of
6 middle-sized seeds.

How many seeds did she plant in all?

Show your thinking.

1 Writing Equations

Write 3 different true equations.

Use 17, 9, and 8 in each equation.

2 Write the Answers

$10 + 30 =$ ___

$20 + 20 =$ ___

$20 + 30 =$ ___

Tell how you know.

3 Choose the Answer

Use 1, 3, and 5. What is the greatest number you can make?

A 351   C 315

B 531   D 513

Explain your thinking.

4 True or False?

$12 +$ ___ $= 26$

The missing number is 13.

Prove it.

1 Building with Blocks

Mario had 100 blocks.
He made a tower with
10 blocks.
He made a wall with
10 blocks.

How many blocks were
left?

Show your thinking.

2 Making 18¢

Draw coins to show
3 different ways to
make 18¢.

3 Write the Answer

$$\begin{array}{r} 40 \\ + 40 \\ \hline \end{array}$$

Tell how you know.

4 Choose the Answer

What number is missing?

13, ___ , 17, 19, 21

○ 14   ○ 11

○ 12   ○ 15

Explain your thinking.

True or False?

Circle T if an equation is true.
Circle F if an equation is false.
If an equation is false, write a correct equation.

1. $6 = 2 + 4$ T   F   _____

2. $6 = 3 + 2$ T   F   _____

3. $6 = 5 + 1$ T   F   _____

4. $8 = 3 + 4$ T   F   _____

5. $8 = 5 + 3$ T   F   _____

6. $8 = 7 + 1$ T   F   _____

7. $10 = 7 + 3$ T   F   _____

8. $10 = 8 + 1$ T   F   _____

9. $10 = 5 + 6$ T   F   _____

10. $10 = 11 - 1$ T   F   _____

11. $10 = 12 - 3$ T   F   _____

12. $10 = 10 - 0$ T   F   _____

Race to the Finish

How fast can you add and subtract numbers in your head?

Start at the bicycle. Race to the finish line.

Add or subtract the numbers along the way.

Write your subtotals in the squares.

Write your total on the finish line.

 $11 - 7 \ \square + 7 \ \square - 4 \ \square + 4 =$ FINISH LINE ___

 $16 + 3 \ \square - 10 \ \square + 8 \ \square + 2 =$ FINISH LINE ___

 $12 + 5 \ \square + 2 \ \square - 3 \ \square - 4 =$ FINISH LINE ___

$9 + 6 \ \square + 3 \ \square - 7 \ \square - 2 =$ FINISH LINE ___

 $17 - 7 \ \square + 3 \ \square + 5 \ \square - 1 =$ FINISH LINE ___

 $14 - 3 \ \square + 5 \ \square + 4 \ \square - 6 =$ FINISH LINE ___

True or False?

2 dimes is the same amount as 3 nickels and 5 pennies.

Prove it.

Checkerboard Squares

There are 32 red squares on a checkerboard. There are 32 black squares, too.

How many squares are there in all?

Show your thinking.

The Answer Is 23¢

Draw coins to show 5 different ways to make 23¢.

Write the Answers

2 + 5 + 5 + 8 = ___

5 + 6 + 5 + 4 = ___

5 + 10 + 5 = ___

Tell how you know.

1 Choose the Answer

Pam has 1 dime, 1 nickel, and 5 pennies. What coin does she need to make 25¢?

A   penny   C   dime

B   quarter   D   nickel

Explain how you know.

2 True or False?

This clock shows 6:15.

Prove it.

3 How Many Hours?

Peter slept from 2 o'clock to 4 o'clock.

How many hours did he sleep?

Show your thinking.

4 The Answer Is 50

Write 2 addition and 2 subtraction equations with this answer.

Name _____

1. Write the Answer

$$50$$
$$+50$$
_____

Tell how you know.

2. Choose the Answer

Which has the same answer as 3 + 4?

A   5 + 3

B   9 − 2

C   2 + 6

D   10 − 4

Explain your thinking.

3. True or False?

37, 47, 57, 67, ___

The next number is 78.

Prove it.

4. How Many Pages?

My book has 200 pages. I read 50 pages.

How many pages are left to read?

Show your thinking.

▼ PARENT NOTE:
Problems like number 1 focus on the ability to add and subtract multiples of 10, an important mental computation skill.

Name _____

How Much?

Count the money.

1.

_____ ¢

2.

_____ ¢

3.

_____ ¢

4.

_____ ¢

5. Which group of coins has the greatest value? _____

6. Which group has the least value? _____

Follow the Trail

Use the arrows to help you find which way to go on the 100 Number Board.

For each trail, begin at the number in the circle.

Follow the trails by moving one square in the direction each arrow points.

At the end of the trail, write the final number you land on in the circle.

1	2	3	4	5	6	7	8	9	10
11	12	13	14	15	16	17	18	19	20
21	22	23	24	25	26	27	28	29	30
31	32	33	34	35	36	37	38	39	40
41	42	43	44	45	46	47	48	49	50
51	52	53	54	55	56	57	58	59	60
61	62	63	64	65	66	67	68	69	70
71	72	73	74	75	76	77	78	79	80
81	82	83	84	85	86	87	88	89	90
91	92	93	94	95	96	97	98	99	100

Begin   End

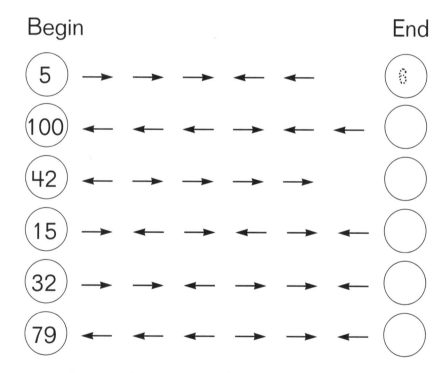

How many numbers do you add or subtract when you move one space this way →? _____ This way ←? _____

1

Write the Answers

$17 + \bigcirc = 20$

$15 + \bigcirc = 18$

$11 + \bigcirc = 19$

Tell how you know.

2

Choose the Answer

$18 - \underline{} = 9$

○ 9

○ 10

○ 8

○ 11

Explain your thinking.

3

True or False?

10 beans and 7 beans
is the same amount as
8 beans and 9 beans.

Prove it.

4

How Many Bears?

3 bears are sleeping
in a cave.
8 bears are out walking.
7 bears are eating berries.

How many bears are there
in all?

Show your thinking.

PARENT NOTE:
One reason *Skill Power* stresses mental computation is this: it is a basic skill for functioning in
an information society in which we *hear* a great deal of the numerical information we receive.

1 Write the Answer

$$16$$
$$+15$$

Tell how you know.

2 The Answer Is 75¢

Draw coins to show
6 different ways to
make 75¢.

3 Choose the Answer

$$17 + 17 = \underline{}$$

A 35

B 34

C 24

D 20

Explain your thinking.

4 True or False?

118 is an odd number.

Prove it.

▼ PARENT NOTE:
Addition and subtraction problems involving two-digit numbers are given for children to solve using their
own reasoning. Children are given appropriate problems and asked what they know to find the answers.

1

Write the Answer

15 + 9 = ____

Tell how you know.

2

Picnic at the Beach

Toni took 6 sandwiches to the beach.

How many people can each have half a sandwich?

Show your thinking.

3

Write the Next 5 Numbers

10, 20, 30, 40, 50,

____ , ____ , ____ ,

____ , ____

Show how you know.

4

Choose the Answer

Which number is less than 49?

A   50

B   39

C   94

D   93

Explain how you know.

How Many Balls?

Ramon had this problem.
There are 2 children.
Each child has 2 balls.
How many balls are there in all?
This is how he did the problem.
What can you say about his work?
Can you think of a way to prove his answer?
Show it.

> There are 2 children each
> child has 2 balls how
> many balls are there in all?
> four. I know because I
> know that two + two = four.

Follow the Trail

Use the arrows to help you find which way to go on the 100 Number Board.

For each trail, begin at the number in the circle.

Follow the trails by moving one square in the direction each arrow points.

At the end of the trail, write the final number you land on in the circle.

1	2	3	4	5	6	7	8	9	10
11	12	13	14	15	16	17	18	19	20
21	22	23	24	25	26	27	28	29	30
31	32	33	34	35	36	37	38	39	40
41	42	43	44	45	46	47	48	49	50
51	52	53	54	55	56	57	58	59	60
61	62	63	64	65	66	67	68	69	70
71	72	73	74	75	76	77	78	79	80
81	82	83	84	85	86	87	88	89	90
91	92	93	94	95	96	97	98	99	100

Begin   End

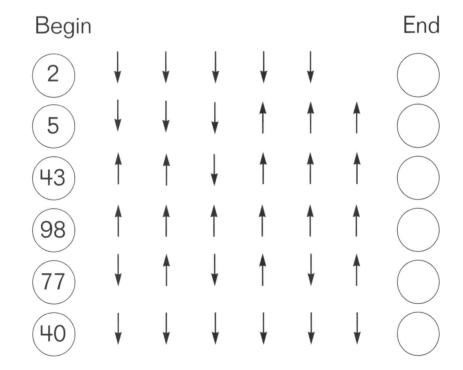

How many numbers do you add or subtract when you move one

space this way ↑ ? _____ This way ↓ ? _____

1

Write the Answers

$$17 \qquad 18 \qquad 19$$
$$\underline{+\,4} \qquad \underline{+\,5} \qquad \underline{+\,6}$$

Tell how you know.

2

True or False?

4 dimes and 5 pennies
is the same amount as
1 quarter, 2 nickels, and
5 pennies.

Prove it.

3

Cups and Spoons

There are 16 cups and
12 spoons.

How many more cups are
there than spoons?

Show your thinking.

4

The Answer Is 60

Write 4 equations that
have this answer.

1
Write the Answers

20	20	20
−10	−11	− 5

Tell how you know.

2
Choose the Answer

$49 =$ ___ + ___

○ 41 + 9

○ 39 + 9

○ 9 + 40

○ 24 + 24

Explain how you know.

3
True or False?

This clock shows 11:15.

Prove it.

4
How Much Gum?

Paul has 5 packs of gum. Each pack of gum has 5 sticks in it.

How many sticks of gum does Paul have?

Show your thinking.

1 Write the Answers

$$10 \atop +10$$ $$10 \atop +15$$ $$15 \atop +15$$

Tell how you know.

2 Write the Answer

How many groups of 6 can you make with 24 shells?

Show your thinking.

3 What Number Comes Next?

31, 33, 35, 37, ___

A   38   C   40

B   39   D   41

Explain how you know.

4 True or False?

3 dimes, 2 nickels, and 5 pennies make 45¢.

Prove it.

What Coins?

What coins could you use to buy the hat?
Draw coins to show 2 different ways.

▼ **PARENT NOTE:**
Solving problems for which the solution is not straightforward, or for which more than one solution is possible, is an important part of *doing* mathematics.

Name _____

Follow the Trail

Use the arrows to help you find which way to go on the 100 Number Board.

For each trail, begin at the number in the circle.

Follow the trails by moving one square in the direction each arrow points.

At the end of the trail, write the final number you land on in the circle.

1	2	3	4	5	6	7	8	9	10
11	12	13	14	15	16	17	18	19	20
21	22	23	24	25	26	27	28	29	30
31	32	33	34	35	36	37	38	39	40
41	42	43	44	45	46	47	48	49	50
51	52	53	54	55	56	57	58	59	60
61	62	63	64	65	66	67	68	69	70
71	72	73	74	75	76	77	78	79	80
81	82	83	84	85	86	87	88	89	90
91	92	93	94	95	96	97	98	99	100

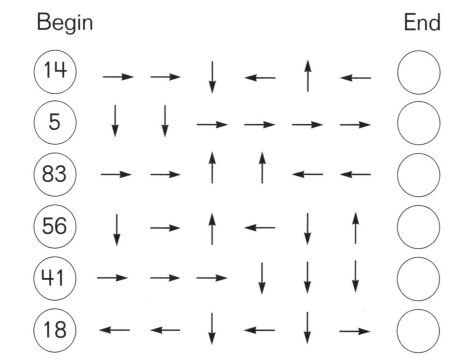

Begin   End

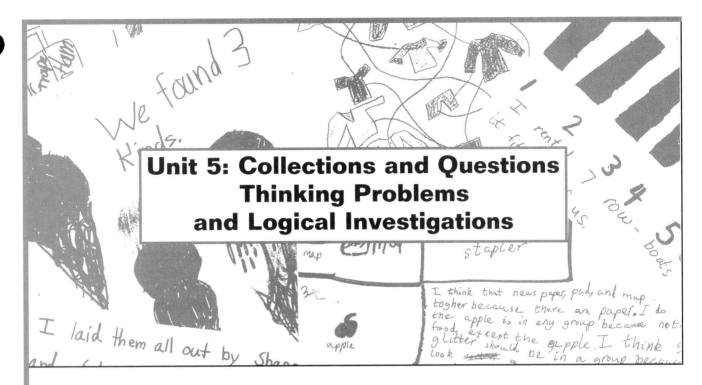

Unit 5: Collections and Questions
Thinking Problems
and Logical Investigations

Thinking Questions

How many ways can you sort attribute pieces? How can you find out where an attribute piece belongs? How can rules help you find the answers to these questions?

Investigations

In this MathLand unit, you will find ways of solving problems with your class. You will discover ways to sort objects based on one or more of their attributes.

Real-World Math

Look at your toys and think about how many ways you can sort them using different rules. Ask members of your family to try to guess your rule. Does your rule help them know what to do?

Math Vocabulary

You will be using these new words to talk about organizing and sorting.

An **attribute** is a characteristic of a person or thing.
Size, shape, and color are attributes.

Example: Some attributes of dogs are shown below.

Spots   Small   Long

To **sort** is to group together things that are alike in some way.

Example: The buttons are sorted into 3 groups.

2 holes   4 holes   No holes

Asking **How many ways ...?** is a good way to find out the possible combinations of things from different groups.

Example: There are 3 flavors of ice cream. How many ways could I order a double-decker cone?

"I found three ways so far."

PARENT NOTE:
The vocabulary pages encourage children to talk about arithmetic problems and concepts in language that makes sense to them. In class, the children will have many opportunities to connect their everyday language to mathematical language and symbols.

Word Practice

Practice writing the math words on the lines below.

large   small   striped   spotted

attributes   _____

   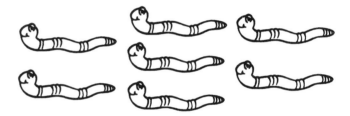

sort   _____

I want to buy 3 of these fish. How many different combinations are possible?

How many ways . . .?   _____

Name _____

Write the Answer

17
+11
——

Tell how you know.

How Many Children?

The children are sitting in 2 rows on the floor. There are 8 children in each row.

How many children are there in all?

Show your thinking.

Write the Answer

Here are two facts in the 5-fact family.

2 + 3 = 5

5 − 3 = 2

Show 2 more facts.

Choose the Answer

What time does this clock show?

A   10:00

B   10:20

C   10:02

D   10:10

Tell how you know.

Write the Answers

14   14   16
+14 +16 +16

Tell how you know.

True or False?

411, 412, 413,

414, _____

The next number is 415.

Prove it.

Magic Beans

Jack had 43 magic beans.
He planted 16 of them.

How many magic beans
did Jack have left?

Show your thinking.

Making 50¢

Draw coins to show
4 different ways
to make 50¢.

Use only dimes and
nickels.

1

Write the Answers

$$\begin{array}{r} 15 \\ +15 \\ \hline \end{array} \qquad \begin{array}{r} 15 \\ +25 \\ \hline \end{array} \qquad \begin{array}{r} 15 \\ +27 \\ \hline \end{array}$$

Tell how you know.

2

Choose the Answer

How much is 6 dimes?

○   10¢

○   25¢

○   60¢

○   50¢

Explain how you know.

3

True or False?

When counting by threes from 33 to 48, you say the number 42.

Prove it.

4

Spare Time

Hyo listened to her radio for 15 minutes.
She listened to tapes for 15 minutes.
Then she watched TV for 30 minutes.

How long did she spend doing these things?

Show your thinking.

▼**PARENT NOTE:**
Throughout *Skill Power*, problems like number 4 are presented so that children can practice using arithmetic in real-life types of situations.

Equations for 8

Randi wrote equations that equal 8.
Here is her work.

$$5 + 3 = 8 \qquad 10 - 2 = 8$$
$$1 + 7 = 8 \qquad 2 - 10 = 8$$
$$0 + 8 = 8 \qquad 11 - 3 = 8$$
$$7 + 1 = 8 \qquad 3 - 11 = 8$$
$$8 + 0 = 8 \qquad 9 - 1 = 8$$
$$3 + 5 = 8 \qquad 1 - 9 = 8$$
$$6 + 2 = 8 \qquad 15 - 7 = 8$$
$$2 + 6 = 8 \qquad 7 - 15 = 8$$
$$4 + 4 = 8 \qquad 16 - 8 = 8$$
$$8 - 16 = 8$$

What can you say about it?

Name _____

Follow the Trail

Use the arrows to help you find which way to go on the 100 Number Board.

For each trail, begin at the number in the circle.

Follow the trails by moving one square in the direction each arrow points.

1	2	3	4	5	6	7	8	9	10
11	12	13	14	15	16	17	18	19	20
21	22	23	24	25	26	27	28	29	30
31	32	33	34	35	36	37	38	39	40
41	42	43	44	45	46	47	48	49	50
51	52	53	54	55	56	57	58	59	60
61	62	63	64	65	66	67	68	69	70
71	72	73	74	75	76	77	78	79	80
81	82	83	84	85	86	87	88	89	90
91	92	93	94	95	96	97	98	99	100

At the end of the trail, write the final number you land on in the circle.

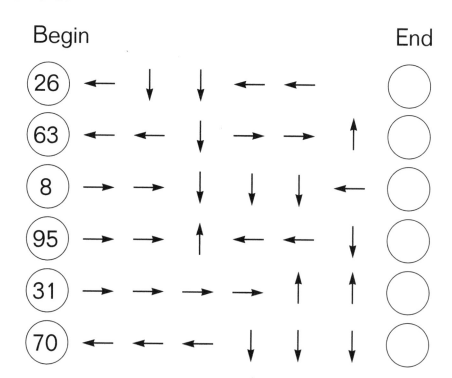

Begin   End

26 ← ↓ ↓ ← ←   ◯

63 ← ← ↓ → → ↑   ◯

8 → → ↓ ↓ ↓ ←   ◯

95 → → ↑ ← ← ↓   ◯

31 → → → → ↑ ↑   ◯

70 ← ← ← ↓ ↓ ↓   ◯

1

Write the Answers

$$\begin{array}{r} 19 \\ +11 \\ \hline \end{array} \qquad \begin{array}{r} 16 \\ +17 \\ \hline \end{array} \qquad \begin{array}{r} 14 \\ +19 \\ \hline \end{array}$$

Tell how you know.

2

Making 75¢

Draw 5 coins that together make 75¢.

3

Choose the Answer

Which number is greater than 386?

A   297

B   368

C   638

D   199

Explain how you know.

4

True or False?

9:15 means half past 9.

Prove it.

1

Write the Answers

25 − 6 = ___

21 − 4 = ___

23 − 5 = ___

Tell how you know.

2

How Many Legs?

There are 15 stools in the room.
Each stool has 3 legs.

How many legs are there in all?

Show your thinking.

3

How Many Groups?

Show how many groups of 3 there are in 15.

4

Choose the Answer

10¢ + 25¢ = ___

A 35¢

B 30¢

C 40¢

D 31¢

Explain how you know.

1

Write the Answers

$$15 \quad\quad 22 \quad\quad 25$$
$$\underline{-5} \quad\quad \underline{-5} \quad\quad \underline{-5}$$

Tell how you know.

2

True or False?

There are 3 groups of 6 in 18.

Prove it.

3

Planting Seeds

Beneta planted carrot seeds in 4 rows. She put 5 seeds in each row.

How many seeds did she plant?

Show your thinking.

4

How to Make 20

Write 4 different numbers you can add to make 20.

Money Questions

Write or draw your answers.

1. José has 3 coins that together make 7¢.
What coins does he have?

2. His brother has 7 coins that together make 7¢.
What coins does he have?

3. Marta has 5 coins that together make 9¢.
What coins does she have?

4. Her sister has 9 coins that together make 9¢.
What coins does she have?

5. Jim has 2 coins that together make 20¢.
What coins does he have?

6. His friend has 3 coins that together make 20¢.
What coins does he have?

7. Piper has 1 coin that makes 25¢.
What coin does she have?

Follow the Trail

For each trail, begin at the number in the circle.

Make trails from the beginning number to the ending number. Draw the arrows to show how you get to the greater number. Use ↑ ↓ → ← .

1	2	3	4	5	6	7	8	9	10
11	12	13	14	15	16	17	18	19	20
21	22	23	24	25	26	27	28	29	30
31	32	33	34	35	36	37	38	39	40
41	42	43	44	45	46	47	48	49	50
51	52	53	54	55	56	57	58	59	60
61	62	63	64	65	66	67	68	69	70
71	72	73	74	75	76	77	78	79	80
81	82	83	84	85	86	87	88	89	90
91	92	93	94	95	96	97	98	99	100

Begin

End

Begin	End
8	68
14	47
72	96
47	80
28	61
63	87

Follow the Trail

For each trail, begin at the number in the circle.

Make trails from the beginning number to the ending number. Draw the arrows to show how you get to the lower number. Use ↑↓ →← .

1	2	3	4	5	6	7	8	9	10
11	12	13	14	15	16	17	18	19	20
21	22	23	24	25	26	27	28	29	30
31	32	33	34	35	36	37	38	39	40
41	42	43	44	45	46	47	48	49	50
51	52	53	54	55	56	57	58	59	60
61	62	63	64	65	66	67	68	69	70
71	72	73	74	75	76	77	78	79	80
81	82	83	84	85	86	87	88	89	90
91	92	93	94	95	96	97	98	99	100

Begin   End

36   12

97   37

9   3

52   19

83   68

44   11

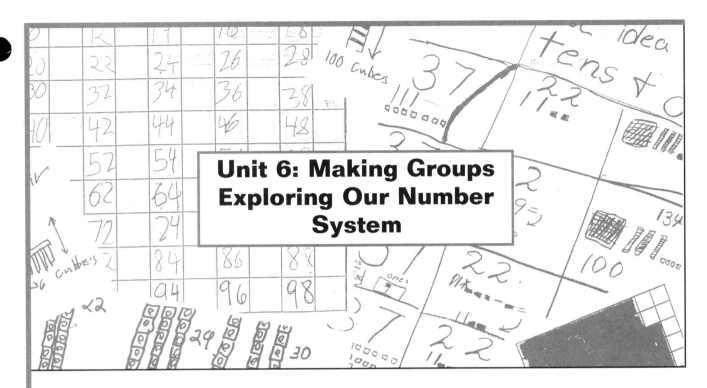

Unit 6: Making Groups Exploring Our Number System

Thinking Questions

How does finding patterns on the 1–100 grid help you fill it in? How many tens and how many ones are in the number 45? How can you use Linker Cubes in ten sticks and ones to measure?

Investigations

In this MathLand unit, you will explore the patterns and relationships in our number system. You will discover ways of using estimating to help you solve problems, and how grouping by 100's, 10's, and 1's can help you count numbers over 100.

Real-World Math

Your home and neighborhood have many examples of the numbers to 100. Finding examples of each number can be an exciting challenge. Groups of things such as Legos, flowers, cars, windows, doors, and food cans can be counted easily. How can grouping by 10's help you as you count?

Math Vocabulary

You will be using these new words to talk about numbers and measurement.

When numbers are in **numerical order,** they are arranged from least to greatest.

| 18 | 4 | 10 | 22 |

| 4 | 10 | 18 | 22 |

Example: Lora put the numbers on the right into numerical order.

To **measure** is to use a tool to find out how long, wide, tall, or heavy something is.

Example: I measured the crayon. It is 5 LinkerCubes long.

An **estimate** is a number that tells *about* how much or how many. To estimate, you use your experience and thinking about numbers.

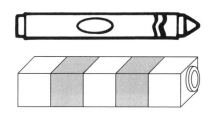

Example: Matt thinks, The table is wider than the desk. The desk is 50 LinkerCubes wide, so I think the table is about 70 LinkerCubes wide.

An object's **length** is how long it is. You can use different tools to measure length.

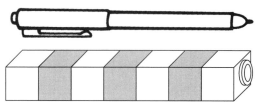

Example: Length = 7 LinkerCubes.

Word Practice

Practice writing the math words on the lines below.

| 3 | 8 | 12 | 19 | 35 | 48 |

numerical order _____

measure _____

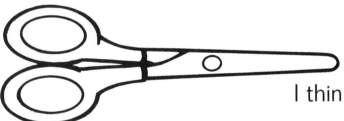

estimate   I think it's about 10 LinkerCubes.

_____

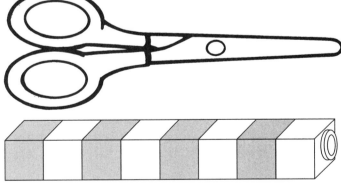

Length = 8 LinkerCubes

length _____

1

Write the Answers

```
  1     3     8
  6     5     4
  9     2     2
 +4    +7    +5
 ───   ───   ───
```

Tell how you know.

2

Choose the Answer

Which number comes just after 389?

- ○ 388
- ○ 390
- ○ 380
- ○ 899

Explain how you know.

3

True or False?

79 is greater than 92.

Prove it.

4

How Many Cars?

Max counted his toy cars. He put them in 4 groups of 4 cars.

How many cars did he have in all?

Show your thinking.

1 Write the Answers

15 + 6 = ___

16 + 8 = ___

18 + 7 = ___

Tell how you know.

2 More Than 10

Show 3 different numbers you can take away from 20 and still have more than 10.

3 Choose the Answer

Which time means 15 minutes past 8?

A   8:18

B   5:15

C   8:30

D   8:15

4 True or False?

___ + 5 = 14

The missing number is 8.

Prove it.

PARENT NOTE:
Children who are encouraged to think logically about computations most often work from left to right, rather than starting from "the ones." This is a natural tendency that shows good thinking about the number system.

Name _____

Write the Answers

$$16 \quad 15 \quad 14$$
$$\underline{-9} \quad \underline{-9} \quad \underline{-9}$$

Tell how you know.

How Many Miles?

A plane flew 100 miles.
Then it flew 300 miles.
Next it flew 200 miles.

How many miles did it fly in all?

Show your thinking.

The Answer Is 80

Write 7 equations that have this answer.

Choose the Answer

Which does not belong in the 11-fact family?

A $5 + 6 = 11$

B $11 + 2 = 13$

C $11 - 5 = 6$

D $11 - 6 = 5$

Explain how you know.

▼ PARENT NOTE:
Children's ability to think about their own thinking, about *how they know*, is an important critical thinking skill. Children often get clearer about their thinking as they tell about it. Take time to read or listen and respond to your child's explanations.

What Number Am I?

1. I am a two-digit number greater than 25.
I have 3 tens and 5 ones.

I am _____ .

2. If you subtract 6 from me, I am 9 tens and 4 ones.

I am _____ .

3. I am a two-digit number less than 91.
My digits are the same.
The sum of my digits is 10.

I am _____ .

4. I have 4 tens.
I am an even number greater than 45.
You say me when you count by fours.

I am _____ .

5. I am greater than 60.
You say me when you count by fives.
The sum of my digits is 12.

I am _____ .

Follow the Trail

For each trail, begin at the number in the circle.

Make the shortest trails possible from the beginning number to the ending number. Draw the arrows to show how you get there. Use ↑ ↓ → ←.

1	2	3	4	5	6	7	8	9	10
11	12	13	14	15	16	17	18	19	20
21	22	23	24	25	26	27	28	29	30
31	32	33	34	35	36	37	38	39	40
41	42	43	44	45	46	47	48	49	50
51	52	53	54	55	56	57	58	59	60
61	62	63	64	65	66	67	68	69	70
71	72	73	74	75	76	77	78	79	80
81	82	83	84	85	86	87	88	89	90
91	92	93	94	95	96	97	98	99	100

Begin   End

39   6

21   45

48   88

87   55

4   18

73   58

PARENT NOTE:
Ask your child to explain how she or he knows a trail is "the shortest trail."

1

Write the Answers

$$\begin{array}{r} 20 \\ +50 \\ \hline \end{array} \quad \begin{array}{r} 80 \\ +20 \\ \hline \end{array} \quad \begin{array}{r} 40 \\ +50 \\ \hline \end{array}$$

Tell how you know.

2

True or False?

One half of 8 is 4.

Prove it.

3

Monkeys in a Tree

19 monkeys are in a tree.
7 are swinging by their tails.
4 are swinging by their hands.

How many monkeys are not swinging at all?

Show your thinking.

4

What Comes Next?

Write the next 4 numbers.

5, 10, 15, 20, ___ ,

___ , ___ , ___

▼ PARENT NOTE:
Mental computation is a challenging activity that builds reasoning skills and number understandings. Children are challenged to solve as many problems in *Skill Power* as they can mentally.

1

Write the Answers

$$\begin{array}{r} 70 \\ -20 \\ \hline \end{array} \qquad \begin{array}{r} 90 \\ -10 \\ \hline \end{array} \qquad \begin{array}{r} 60 \\ -50 \\ \hline \end{array}$$

Tell how you know.

2

Choose the Answer

What is the least number you can make?

Use the numbers 8, 4, 3, and 2.

A   3842   C   2348

B   3428   D   4328

Explain how you know.

3

True or False?

One-half hour is the same as 30 minutes.

Prove it.

4

Toy Cars

Toy cars cost 5¢ each.
Sean has 18¢.
His mother gives him 2¢ more.

How many toy cars can Sean buy?

Show your thinking.

1 Write the Answers

68   46   77
−5   −4   −6

Tell how you know.

2 Which Group Has More?

Draw 7 groups of 4 things. Now draw 4 groups of 7 things.

Tell which set of groups has more.

3 Choose the Answer

Which time means 12 minutes after 12?

○ 12:10

○ 12:02

○ 1:12

○ 12:12

Explain how you know.

4 True or False?

3, 6, and 10 are all even numbers.

Prove it.

Name _____

100 Number Board

Write the missing numbers on the hundred number chart.
Tell about the number patterns you see.

1	2	3							10
11			14	15		17	18		
	22		24		26			29	30
31				35		37			
	42		44	45			48	49	
51					56				60
	62		64	65			68	69	
71					76	77			80
		84		86				89	
	92	93				97			100

Follow the Trail

You can use arrow trails on the 100 Number Board to help solve addition problems.

1	2	3	4	5	6	7	8	9	10
11	12	13	14	15	16	17	18	19	20
21	22	23	24	25	26	27	28	29	30
31	32	33	34	35	36	37	38	39	40
41	42	43	44	45	46	47	48	49	50
51	52	53	54	55	56	57	58	59	60
61	62	63	64	65	66	67	68	69	70
71	72	73	74	75	76	77	78	79	80
81	82	83	84	85	86	87	88	89	90
91	92	93	94	95	96	97	98	99	100

Katja said, "Here's how I solved 15 + 12 using an arrow trail."

15 ↓ → → 27

Do you agree that her way works?

Make arrow trails to solve the problems below.

Use ↑ ↓ → ← to record your trails. Write the sum in the circle at the end.

Begin   End

10 + 40   ◯

5 + 51   ◯

42 + 17   ◯

73 + 21   ◯

1 + 99   ◯

▼ PARENT NOTE:
Experiences with the 100 Number Board help children understand number sequence as well as how to visualize addition and subtraction with two-digit numbers.

Name _____

Write the Answer

8
+62

Tell how you know.

Making Shoes

An elf was making
8 shoes.
He pounded 6 nails into
each shoe.

How many nails did he
pound in all?

Show your thinking.

The Answer Is 85

Write 8 equations that
have this answer.

Choose the Answer

How much is 4 fours?

A   More than 15

B   Less than 14

C   Exactly 20

D   Between 10 and 15

Explain how you know.

Name _____

Write the Answer

16 − 6 = ___

Tell how you know.

True or False?

528 is greater than 482.

Prove it.

Space Creatures

On Mars there were 12 moon men, 11 aliens, and 10 little green men.

How many creatures were there in all?

Show your thinking.

Write the Answer

What numbers are missing?

9 + 5 = ___

5 + ___ = 14

___ − 5 = 9

14 − ___ = 5

Tell how you know.

1 ▼

Write the Answer

18 − 9 = ___

Tell how you know.

2 ▼

Choose the Answer

25 − 19 = ___

A   5

B   4

C   6

D   14

Explain your thinking.

3 ▼

True or False?

500 comes after 450 and before 611.

Prove it.

4 ▼

How Many Eggs?

There are 12 eggs in 1 dozen.

How many eggs are there in 10 dozen?

Show your thinking.

In Order

Write the numbers in order from least to greatest.

| 20 | 4 | 16 | 11 | 2 | 18 |

1. ____ ____ ____ ____ ____ ____

| 34 | 17 | 40 | 81 | 50 | 45 |

2. ____ ____ ____ ____ ____ ____

| 203 | 111 | 300 | 212 | 481 | 501 |

3. ____ ____ ____ ____ ____ ____

| 499 | 302 | 198 | 500 | 260 | 386 |

4. ____ ____ ____ ____ ____ ____

Follow the Trail

You can use arrow trails on the 100 Number Board to help solve subtraction problems.

Ari said, "Here's how I solved 67 − 13 using an arrow trail."

67 ↑ ← ← ← 54

Do you agree that his way works?

1	2	3	4	5	6	7	8	9	10
11	12	13	14	15	16	17	18	19	20
21	22	23	24	25	26	27	28	29	30
31	32	33	34	35	36	37	38	39	40
41	42	43	44	45	46	47	48	49	50
51	52	53	54	55	56	57	58	59	60
61	62	63	64	65	66	67	68	69	70
71	72	73	74	75	76	77	78	79	80
81	82	83	84	85	86	87	88	89	90
91	92	93	94	95	96	97	98	99	100

Make arrow trails to solve the problems below.

Use ↑↓ → ← to record your trails. Write the difference in the circle at the end.

Begin   End

27 − 22

66 − 33

8 − 7

34 − 17

83 − 23

92 − 50

Name _____

Write the Answer

$$
\begin{array}{r}
9 \\
7 \\
4 \\
+2 \\
\hline
\end{array}
$$

Tell how you know.

2

Making 85¢

Draw 3 coins that together make 85¢.

 3

Choose the Answer

Which number is closest to 641?

○ 541

○ 640

○ 638

○ 650

Explain how you know.

 4

True or False?

$1.00 is less than 99¢.

Prove it.

▼ **PARENT NOTE:**
When children write about their strategies, they have the chance to explain their thinking and to practice communicating their ideas to others.

1

Write the Answer

128 + 4 = ___

Tell how you know.

2

Snow White

Snow White and
the 7 dwarfs came
walking along.
Each one had 3 apples.

How many apples did they
have in all?

Show your thinking.

3

What Is the Answer?

```
  16
  15
   4
+ 10
```

Use pictures, words, or
numbers to explain your
thinking.

4

Choose the Answer

Skip count by fours. Which
number did you not say?

A 9   C 4

B 8   D 12

Tell how you know.

▼ **PARENT NOTE:**
Support your child's natural inclination to take care of the big numbers first when adding and subtracting
(rather than to "start with the ones"). This models successful strategies for estimation and mental arithmetic.

1

Write the Answers

$$100 \qquad 100$$
$$+ \ 6 \qquad + 60$$

Tell how you know.

2

True or False?

7:15 is the same as a quarter past 7.

Prove it.

3

Paper Folding

Gayla and her friends were paper folding. They folded 17 paper cranes. They folded 17 horses and 6 cats.

How many animals did they fold in all?

Show your thinking.

4

The Answer Is 68

Write 7 equations that have this answer. Can you write more?

What Comes?

What number comes just after?

1. 161 _____

2. 383 _____

3. 206 _____

4. 449 _____

What number comes just before?

5. _____ 58

6. _____ 39

7. _____ 600

8. _____ 411

Follow the Trail

You can use arrow trails on the 100 Number Board to help solve addition and subtraction problems.

Make arrow trails to solve the problems below. Use ↑↓→←.
Record your trails and the sums and differences.

1	2	3	4	5	6	7	8	9	10
11	12	13	14	15	16	17	18	19	20
21	22	23	24	25	26	27	28	29	30
31	32	33	34	35	36	37	38	39	40
41	42	43	44	45	46	47	48	49	50
51	52	53	54	55	56	57	58	59	60
61	62	63	64	65	66	67	68	69	70
71	72	73	74	75	76	77	78	79	80
81	82	83	84	85	86	87	88	89	90
91	92	93	94	95	96	97	98	99	100

Begin   End

$19 - 13$ ◯

$100 - 25$ ◯

$4 + 51$ ◯

$62 - 16$ ◯

$12 + 64$ ◯

$25 + 53$ ◯

▼ PARENT NOTE:
Ask your child to tell you if there is a way to tell which trails are like subtraction and which like addition by looking only at the trails.

1 Write the Answer

14
+ 36
———

Tell how you know.

2 Choose the Answer

Which time means
5 minutes after 8?

○ 8:05

○ 8:50

○ 8:08

○ 5:08

Explain your thinking.

3 True or False?

367 comes between 374
and 379.

Prove it.

4 How Much Money?

Maia had 1 quarter,
2 dimes, and 4 pennies.
She spent 37¢.

How much money did she
have left?

Show your thinking.

1. Write the Answer

$$
\begin{array}{r}
3 \\
9 \\
11 \\
7 \\
+\ 8 \\
\hline
\end{array}
$$

Tell how you know.

2. How Many?

Sasha has 3 bunches of 17 flowers. How many flowers is that in all.

Use pictures, words, or numbers to tell about your thinking.

3. Choose the Answer

Which number is less than 243?

A   239   C   244

B   251   D   423

Explain how you know.

4. True or False?

3 is one half of 9.

Prove it.

PARENT NOTE:
One of the most important ideas that children can learn is that a problem usually has one correct answer but more than one strategy for getting that answer.

1

Write the Answer

$$400 - 200 = \underline{\hspace{1cm}}$$

Tell how you know.

2

How Many Newspapers?

Placi had 25 newspapers to deliver.
He stacked them in piles of 5 papers.

How many stacks were there?

Show your thinking.

3

The Answer Is 100

Write 8 equations that have this answer.

4

Choose the Answer

Which number comes just before 426?

A 427

B 425

C 325

D 435

Explain how you know.

My Numbers

Write the numbers on the lines.

1. ten _____

2. twenty-five _____

3. thirty-one _____

4. forty-two _____

5. sixty-eight _____

6. one hundred three _____

Name _____

Follow the Trail

Use arrow trails on the 100 Number Board to help find the shortest trails possible in these addition and subtraction problems.

Use ↑↓ →←. Record your trails and the sums and differences.

1	2	3	4	5	6	7	8	9	10
11	12	13	14	15	16	17	18	19	20
21	22	23	24	25	26	27	28	29	30
31	32	33	34	35	36	37	38	39	40
41	42	43	44	45	46	47	48	49	50
51	52	53	54	55	56	57	58	59	60
61	62	63	64	65	66	67	68	69	70
71	72	73	74	75	76	77	78	79	80
81	82	83	84	85	86	87	88	89	90
91	92	93	94	95	96	97	98	99	100

Begin   End

$97 - 49$ ◯

$14 + 14$ ◯

$57 + 26$ ◯

$71 - 15$ ◯

$11 + 12$ ◯

$13 - 12$ ◯

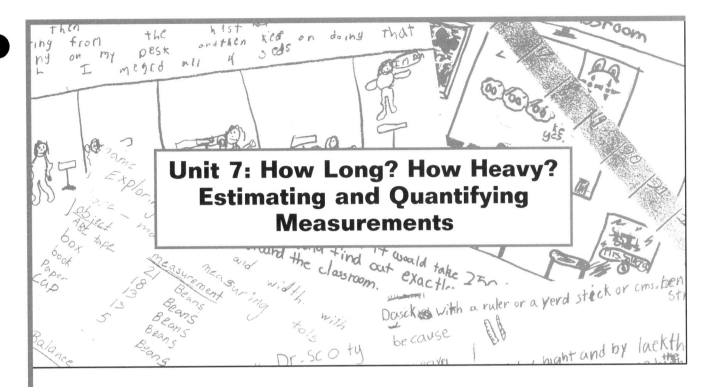

Unit 7: How Long? How Heavy? Estimating and Quantifying Measurements

Thinking Questions

Why is estimating helpful when you are weighing and measuring things? Can you change your estimate if you get more information? How might you create your own measuring tools?

Investigations

In this MathLand unit, you will practice estimating before you weigh and measure things with a measuring tool you have made yourself. You also will learn how to adjust your estimate so that it reflects your new ideas.

Real-World Math

Estimation is used all the time in our daily lives. A fisherman estimates how much bait he will need for the time he is fishing. A cook estimates how much food to buy for the customers. What are some real-life estimates you can make that will help you make decisions?

Math Vocabulary

You will be using these new words in this unit to talk about measuring.

A **balance scale** is a tool used to find out how heavy things are.

Example: It takes 30 beans to balance the eraser on the balance scale.

Weight = 152 beans
Height = 36 beans
Girth = 29 beans

An object's **weight** is how heavy it is.

An object's **height** is how tall it is from top to bottom.

An object's **girth** is how big around it is.

Weight = 152 beans

Height = 36 beans

Girth = 29 beans

An **inch** is a unit of length used to measure objects.

Area is the amount of space a shape takes up.

Example: The area of the shape is 25 beans.

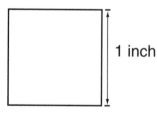

1 inch

Word Practice

Practice writing the math words on the lines below.

balance scale
_____

weight

height

girth

Weight = 16 beans
Height = 12 beans
Girth = 8 beans

_____

_____

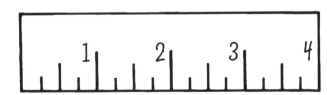

inch
_____

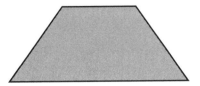 

area
_____

1. Write the Answers

$$110 \atop +\ 10 \over $$ $$110 \atop +\ 40 \over $$

Tell how you know.

2. True or False?

507 comes between 506 and 508.

Prove it.

3. How Many Train Cars?

Pepe had lots of cars for his train.
He put them in 8 groups of 3 cars each.

How many train cars did he have?

Show your thinking.

4. The Answer Is 47

Write 4 addition and 4 subtraction equations that have this answer.
Can you think of more?

PARENT NOTE:
Presenting numbers that are easy to think about (as in number 1) helps children to realize they can work with big numbers. With your child, take turns making up big-number problems to solve. Keep the numbers in the easy-to-think-about range.

1

Write the Answer

$$
\begin{array}{r}
13 \\
7 \\
12 \\
+\ 5 \\
\hline
\end{array}
$$

Tell how you know.

2

Choose the Answer

$8 - \underline{} = 3$

A   3

B   6

C   5

D   11

Explain how you know.

3

True or False?

4 quarters make $2.50.

Prove it.

4

Recess Time

In the yard 15 children were running.
12 were jumping rope.
13 were playing ball.

How many children were playing in the yard?

Show your thinking.

1. Write the Answer

16 − 7 = ___

Tell how you know.

2. How Many Groups?

Draw a picture to show that 4 groups of 5 is the same as 5 groups of 4.

How many is it in all?

3. Choose the Answer

Where would you look for the missing number?

28 + ___ = 40

○ 22   ○ 13

○ 12   ○ 23

Explain your thinking.

4. True or False?

A dollar is 10¢ more than 3 quarters.

Prove it.

Measure, Measure

Look around at home or at school.
Find some things that measure about the same length as each thing listed.

1. What is as long as this piece of paper?

_____

2. What is as wide as this piece of paper?

_____

3. What is as long as your thumb?

_____

4. What is as long as your foot?

_____

5. What is as long as a book or magazine?

_____

6. What is as long as a big piece of newspaper?

_____

Follow the Trail

Erica said, "Sometimes it's shorter to use some subtraction to solve addition problems." I did $43 + 19$ this way: ↓ ↓ ←.

Make the shortest arrow trails possible to solve the problems below. Use ↑ ↓ → ←. Record your trails and the sums and differences.

1	2	3	4	5	6	7	8	9	10
11	12	13	14	15	16	17	18	19	20
21	22	23	24	25	26	27	28	29	30
31	32	33	34	35	36	37	38	39	40
41	42	43	44	45	46	47	48	49	50
51	52	53	54	55	56	57	58	59	60
61	62	63	64	65	66	67	68	69	70
71	72	73	74	75	76	77	78	79	80
81	82	83	84	85	86	87	88	89	90
91	92	93	94	95	96	97	98	99	100

Begin   End

$82 + 17$ ◯

$58 - 32$ ◯

$20 - 18$ ◯

$3 + 34$ ◯

$95 - 42$ ◯

$29 + 43$ ◯

Write the Answers

9 + 13 = ___

9 + 23 = ___

9 + 33 = ___

Tell how you know.

How Many Puppets?

Jan had 16 puppets.
She got 2 more for her birthday.
She gave away 4 puppets to a friend.

How many puppets did she have then?

Show your thinking.

Write the Answer

Would you rather have 120 pennies or $1.10?

Use pictures, words, or numbers to explain your thinking.

Choose the Answer

Which is not in the 11-fact family?

A   5 + 6 = 11

B   11 − 5 = 6

C   6 + 5 = 11

D   11 − 6 = 6

Explain how you know.

PARENT NOTE:
To solve addition and subtraction problems, a child may use a few strategies over and over. Children add new strategies gradually, as their thinking and number sense develop.

1

Write the Answer

$$120 - 20 = \underline{\qquad}$$

Tell how you know.

2

True or False?

12 books in 4 equal groups is 3 books in each group.

Prove it.

3

At the Beach

8 beach balls were in the water.
14 beach balls were on the sand.
2 beach balls were rolling away.

How many beach balls were there in all?

Show your thinking.

4

Dividing a Square

Draw a square. Show 2 different ways to divide the square in half.

Name _____

1

Write the Answers

$15 - 6 =$ ____

$25 - 6 =$ ____

$35 - 6 =$ ____

Tell how you know.

2

Choose the Answer

____ $- 8 = 4$

A 12

B 11

C 10

D 14

Explain how you know.

3

True or False?

$1.57 is the same as 6 quarters.

Prove it.

4

Diving Deep

A diver went 10 feet under water.
Then she came up 3 feet.
Next she went down 6 feet.

How many feet under water was she then?

Show your thinking.

What Time?

1. It is 1 o'clock. What time will it be in 1 hour?

_____ o'clock

2. It is 7 o'clock. What time will it be in 1 hour?

_____ o'clock

3. It is 9:30. What time will it be in half an hour?

_____ o'clock

4. It is 4:30. What time will it be in 1 hour?

_____ : _____

5. It is 6 o'clock. What time will it be in 15 minutes?

_____ : _____

6. It is 11:30. What time will it be in 15 minutes?

_____ : _____

Follow the Trail

Use arrow trails on the 100 Number Board to help find the shortest trails in these addition and subtraction problems.

Make the shortest arrow trails possible to solve the problems below. Use ↑ ↓ → ←. Record your trails and the sums and differences.

1	2	3	4	5	6	7	8	9	10
11	12	13	14	15	16	17	18	19	20
21	22	23	24	25	26	27	28	29	30
31	32	33	34	35	36	37	38	39	40
41	42	43	44	45	46	47	48	49	50
51	52	53	54	55	56	57	58	59	60
61	62	63	64	65	66	67	68	69	70
71	72	73	74	75	76	77	78	79	80
81	82	83	84	85	86	87	88	89	90
91	92	93	94	95	96	97	98	99	100

Begin   End

$36 + 41$

$7 + 62$

$35 - 26$

$79 - 16$

$91 - 27$

$45 + 45$

Name _____

Write the Answer

$$
\begin{array}{r}
8 \\
6 \\
3 \\
11 \\
+\ 4 \\
\hline
\end{array}
$$

Tell how you know.

Making 75¢

Draw 6 coins that together make 75¢.

Choose the Answer

$13 - \underline{} = 9$

○ 5

○ 6

○ 4

○ 12

Explain how you know.

True or False?

This clock shows 11:25.

Prove it.

1

Write the Answer

$$16$$
$$- \ 9$$

Tell how you know.

2

Pets

Luisa fed her 3 cats and 2 dogs in the morning.

She fed 19 fish and 12 rabbits at night.

How many pets does Luisa have in all?

Show your thinking.

3

Write the Answer

What numbers are missing?

$6 + \_\_\_ = 12$

$7 + 7 = \_\_\_$

$\_\_\_ + 8 = 16$

$9 + 9 = \_\_\_$

4

Choose the Answer

What number comes just before 1000?

A   1001

B   900

C   999

D   998

Tell how you know.

1

Write the Answer

20 − 7 = ___

Tell how you know.

2

True or False?

2 quarters and 2 dimes make 80¢ in all.

Prove it.

3

How Many Shells?

Masao put his shells in 6 rows.
There were 5 shells in each row.
How many shells did Masao have?

Show your thinking.

4

What Comes Between?

Write 4 numbers that come between 539 and 547.

▼PARENT NOTE:
Try solving some problems yourself using mental computation and noticing the different ways you approach problems.

Calendar Trivia

May

Sun.	Mon.	Tues.	Wed.	Thurs.	Fri.	Sat.
	1	2	3	4	5	6
7	8	9	10	11	12	13
14	15	16	17	18	19	20
21	22	23	24	25	26	27
28	29	30	31			

1. How many days are there in 1 week? _____

2. How many days are there in May? _____

3. How many whole weeks are there this month? _____

4. How many Sundays are there this month? _____

5. How many Wednesdays are there this month? _____

6. What day is May 1 this month? _____

Name _____

What's My Rule?

This is UDRF. UDRF has a built-in computer system. When you put a number in, it sends a number out. Figure out UDRF's computer's secret rule for each table. Write the missing numbers in the table. Then write the rule.

In

Out

In	Out
3	6
10	13
5	8
9	12
6	9
1	4

The rule is _____add 3_____ .

In	Out
8	18
2	12
4	14
7	
1	
10	

The rule is _____ .

In	Out
11	6
7	2
9	4
10	
5	
8	

The rule is _____ .

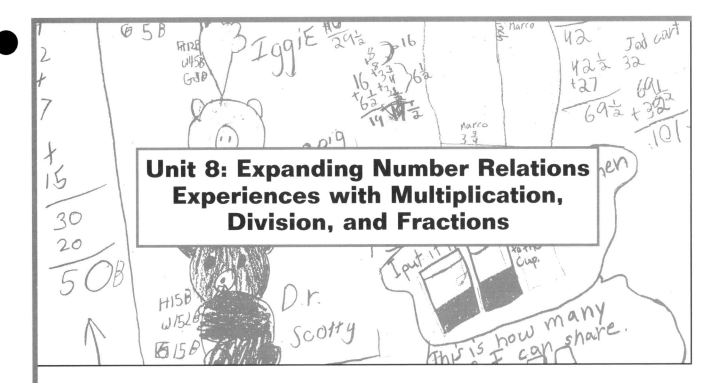

Unit 8: Expanding Number Relations
Experiences with Multiplication, Division, and Fractions

Thinking Questions

How do you begin finding number pairs for a large number? How are you sure you have found all the pairs? Is there a way to organize and record your equations that will help you find all the pairs?

Investigations

In this MathLand unit, you will find the answers to these questions. You will be adding and subtracting two-digit numbers and estimating, measuring, and comparing. You will also use skip counting and repeated addition to combine equal groups.

Real-World Math

Sharing cookies with your brothers and sisters or toys with your friends are everyday problems. Deciding how to do that fairly is not easy if there isn't enough to divide equally. What do you do when everyone cannot have an equal share?

Math Vocabulary

You will be using these new words to talk about groups of numbers.

A **number pair** is a group of two numbers that equal a certain sum.

| 10 + 5 | 7 + 8 | 6 + 9 |

Example: Here are some number pairs for 15.

| 13 − 9 = 4 | 12 + 8 = 20 |

An **equation** is a number sentence.
It has equal values on both sides of an equal sign.

Equal groups are bunches of the same number of objects.
You can use equal groups to help you think about number problems.

Example: How many fingers are on 3 hands?

3 equal groups of 5 fingers = 15 fingers

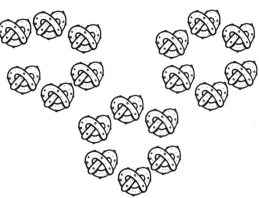

Each friend's fair share is 6 pretzels.

Fair shares is a way of dividing something into equal groups.

Example: Three friends want fair shares of 18 pretzels.

How many should each friend get?

Word Practice

Practice writing the math words on the lines below.

| 0 + 8 | 1 + 7 | 2 + 6 | 3 + 5 |

number pairs _____

| 18 + 7 = 25 | 30 − 2 = 28 |

equation _____

equal groups _____

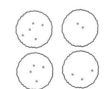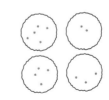

fair shares _____

Write the Answer

8 + 18 = ___

Tell how you know.

Choose the Answer

What number comes just before 500?

○ 400

○ 499

○ 501

○ 449

Explain how you know.

True or False?

428 is the greatest number you can make using the numerals 2, 4, and 8.

Prove it.

At the Beach

Sai picked up 29 shells on the beach.
He put back 16 of them.
Then he picked up 14 bright pebbles.

How many shells and pebbles did he have?

Show your thinking.

1

Write the Answer

100 + 100 = _____

Tell how you know.

2

Draw a Circle

Show a way to cut your circle in half.

3

Choose the Answer

200 is how much more than 100?

A   50

B   150

C   200

D   100

Explain your thinking.

4

True or False?

4 half dollars make $2.50.

Prove it.

1 Write the Answer

$$\begin{array}{r} 200 \\ -100 \\ \hline \end{array}$$

Tell how you know.

2 Let's Play!

There were 53 children on the playground. 48 of them came inside after 10 minutes.

How many children were left on the playground?

Show your thinking.

3 The Answer Is 52

Write 8 equations that have this answer. Write more if you would like.

4 Choose the Answer

50 is half of what number?

A   100

B   200

C   150

D   25

Explain how you know.

What's the Number?

Use these numerals to make numbers that answer the questions.

1. What number comes after 26? _____

2. What number comes before 83? _____

3. What number comes between 48 and 50? _____

4. What number is 3 more than 789? _____

5. What is the least number you can make? _____

6. What number comes after 278? _____

7. What number comes before 298? _____

8. What number comes between 741 and 743? _____

What's My Rule?

This is UDRF. UDRF has a built-in computer system. When you put a number in, it sends a number out. Figure out UDRF's computer's secret rule for each table. Write the missing numbers in the table. Then write the rule.

In	Out
17	14
12	9
14	11
15	
10	
13	

The rule is _____.

In	Out
2	10
5	13
7	15
4	
9	
12	

The rule is _____.

In	Out
20	16
15	11
16	12
4	
18	
13	

The rule is _____.

① Write the Answers

28 + 17 = ___

27 + 18 = ___

17 + 28 = ___

Tell how you know.

② True or False?

Ten plus ten has the same answer as fifteen plus five.

Prove it.

③ The Dog Show

There were 9 dogs in the dog show.
Each dog had 3 dishes for food and water.

How many dishes were there?

Show your thinking.

④ What Makes $1.00?

Draw 4 coins that together make $1.00.

▼ **PARENT NOTE:**
Support your child's natural inclination to take care of the big numbers first when adding and subtracting (rather than to "start with the ones"). This models successful strategies for estimation and mental arithmetic.

Write the Answers

$$35 \atop +10$$ $$35 \atop +30$$ $$45 \atop +30$$

Tell how you know.

Choose the Answer

17 is how much more than 8?

A   5

B   11

C   9

D   10

Explain how you know.

The Answer Is 25

Write 3 addition equations and 3 subtraction equations that have this answer.

How Many Pictures?

There are 9 pages in Paula's book.
Paula has 36 pictures.
She wants to put the same number of pictures on each page.

How many pictures will Paula put on each page?

Show your thinking.

1

Write the Answers

$$\begin{array}{r} 25 \\ -20 \\ \hline \end{array} \qquad \begin{array}{r} 47 \\ -10 \\ \hline \end{array} \qquad \begin{array}{r} 63 \\ -50 \\ \hline \end{array}$$

Tell how you know.

 **2**

Write the Answers

How many 3-digit numbers can you make?

Use the numerals 3, 7, and 8 in each number.

 3

Choose the Answer

Skip count by sixes. Which number did you not say?

○ 11

○ 12

○ 6

○ 18

Explain how you know.

 4

True or False?

3 groups of 5 is equal to 12.

Prove it.

A Subtraction Problem

Amanda had this problem.

$$15 - 3 = \underline{}$$

I kNew That 15 – 2 was 12
and 15 – 4 = Was 10. So I asKed my
Self whats in The Middle
of 10 and 12 and it was 11.

15 – 3 = 11

How would you do the problem?

Tell about your way.

Did you get the same answer Amanda got?

▼ PARENT NOTE:
Children's ability to think about their own thinking, about *how they know,* is an important critical-thinking skill. Children often get clearer about their thinking as they tell about it. Take time to read, listen, and respond to your child's explanations.

What's My Rule?

This is UDRF. UDRF has a built-in computer system. When you put a number in, it sends a number out. Figure out UDRF's computer's secret rule for each table. Write the missing numbers in the table. Then write the rule.

In	Out
6	8
12	14
5	7
0	
9	
18	

The rule is _____.

In	Out
3	6
8	11
4	7
11	
2	
10	

The rule is _____.

In	Out
18	11
9	2
11	4
8	
13	
10	

The rule is _____.

▼ **PARENT NOTE:**
Children feel powerful when they figure out a "secret rule." Encourage your child to talk about the thought processes used to figure out the secret rule.

1

Write the Answer

$$45$$
$$-10$$

Tell how you know.

2

Balloons for Sale

The balloon man had
65 balloons.
He sold 19 of them.
He pumped up 15 more.

How many balloons did he
have then?

Show your thinking.

3

Write the Answer

What numbers are
missing?

$7 + \underline{\quad} = 13$

$\underline{\quad} - 6 = 7$

$13 - 7 = \underline{\quad}$

$\underline{\quad} + 7 = 13$

4

How Many Minutes?

Erika worked for
27 minutes and rested
for 5 minutes.
Then she worked for
20 more minutes.

How many minutes did
she work in all?

Write an equation to solve
this problem.

1 ▼

Write the Answer

$$
\begin{array}{r}
33 \\
+19 \\
\hline
\end{array}
$$

Tell how you know.

2 ▼

True or False?

3 dimes are worth more than 2 quarters.

Prove it.

3 ▼

How Many Flowers?

There were 11 jars on a window sill.
Each jar had 4 flowers in it.

How many flowers were there in all?

Show your thinking.

4 ▼

The Answer Is 24

Write at least 7 equations that have this answer.

1

Write the Answer

154 + 20 = _____

Tell how you know.

2

Choose the Answer

Which number is greater than 821?

○ 805   ○ 812

○ 831   ○ 820

Explain how you know.

3

True or False?

25 is half of 75.

Prove it.

4

Tiles in a Pattern

Deepak wants to put 28 tiles in a pattern. He is going to put 7 tiles in each row.

How many rows of tiles will Deepak have?

Show your thinking.

Groups Of

1. Draw 3 groups of 3 small squares.

How many squares in all? ____

2. Draw 4 groups of 3 triangles.

How many triangles in all? ____

3. Draw 3 groups of 4 small circles.

How many circles in all? ____

4. Draw 4 groups of 2 houses.

How many houses in all? ____

What's My Rule?

This is UDRF. UDRF has a built-in computer system. When you put a number in, it sends a number out. Figure out UDRF's computer's secret rule for each table. Write the missing numbers in the table. Then write the rule.

In

Out

In	Out
3	12
5	14
8	17
1	
4	
2	

The rule is _____.

In	Out
4	8
9	13
2	6
1	
5	
3	

The rule is _____.

In	Out
20	18
14	12
17	15
13	
7	
4	

The rule is _____.

Write the Answer

17
4
29
5
+ 3
___

Tell how you know.

Show the Time

Draw 6:15 on this clock.

Choose the Answers

Which two are equal to each other?

A   12 + 6

B   11 + 6

C   20 − 2

D   18 − 3

Explain how you know.

True or False?

3 groups of 11 is 33.

Prove it.

Name _____

Write the Answer

125
−15
―――

Tell how you know.

The Ants Go Marching

7 ants came marching to the picnic.
Each ant carried away 5 crumbs.

How many crumbs did they take in all?

Show your thinking.

The Answer Is 10

Write 10 equations that have this answer. Can you think of more?

Choose the Answer

Which skip-counting pattern is not correct?

A   2, 4, 6, 8, 10

B   1, 3, 5, 7, 9

C   5, 10, 15, 20, 25

D   10, 20, 25, 30, 40

Explain how you know.

▼—**PARENT NOTE:**—
Children can explore the meanings of multiplication and division in story situations like number 2 in preparation for later work with written equations.

Write the Answer

25
+ 7

Tell how you know.

True or False?

13 + 15 has the same answer as 14 + 14.

Prove it.

How Many Phone Calls?

Joscelyn made 6 phone calls in 1 week.
Her brother made 5 calls.
Their mother made 18 calls.
Their father made 12 calls.

How many calls did the family make in all?

Show your thinking.

The Answer Is 101

Write 9 equations that have this answer.

More Groups

1. Draw 12 small squares.
   Show how you would put them into
   2 equal groups.

2. Draw 12 small circles.
   Show how you would put them into
   3 equal groups.

3. Draw 12 small rectangles.
   Show how you would put them into
   4 equal groups.

4. Draw 12 small triangles.
   Show how you would put them into
   6 equal groups.

What's My Rule?

This is UDRF. UDRF has a built-in computer system. When you put a number in, it sends a number out. Figure out UDRF's computer's secret rule for each table. Write the missing numbers in the table. Then write the rule.

In	Out
12	17
9	14
1	6
5	
9	
19	

The rule is _____.

In	Out
16	27
9	20
12	23
15	
11	
20	

The rule is _____.

In	Out
14	8
17	11
9	3
12	
10	
19	

The rule is _____.

1 Write the Answer

$127 + 3 =$ _____

Tell how you know.

2 Choose the Answer

How much is 3 quarters and 1 penny?

A   75¢

B   76¢

C   51¢

D   74¢

Explain how you know.

3 True or False?

250, 205, 502, 520

502 is the greatest of these numbers.

Prove it.

4 Yummy Muffins

Mrs. Chavez baked 2 pans of muffins.
There were 6 muffins in each pan.

How many children can each have 2 muffins?

Show your thinking.

PARENT NOTE:
Children have many experiences with sharing before they enter school. Story problems like number 4 invite children to connect what they already know to the thinking they do in school arithmetic.

1

Write the Answer

38
−13

Tell how you know.

2

The Answer Is 75¢

Draw coins to show
6 different ways to
make 75¢.

3

Choose the Answer

Which time means half
past 4?

○ 4:30

○ 4:40

○ 4:20

○ 4:15

Explain how you know.

4

True or False?

Ten take away six plus
eleven is fifteen.

Prove it.

Name _____

Write the Answers

116 + 4 = _____

114 + 6 = _____

Tell how you know.

Rainy Day

20 people were out
in the rain.
12 people ran for cover.
6 others had umbrellas.

How many people got wet
in the rain?

Show your thinking.

Sharing Sandwiches

How could 6 children
share 3 sandwiches
equally?

Use pictures, words, or
numbers to explain your
thinking.

Choose the Answer

4 girls each have 75¢.
How much do they have
in all?

A $1.00   C $3.00

B $2.00   D $4.00

Explain how you know.

▼ PARENT NOTE:
Children can use visual thinking and reasoning to solve most problems that involve fractions commonly used
in everyday living.

Equal Parts

Divide each square into equal parts.

1.

2 parts

4.

3 parts

2.

4 parts

5.

4 parts (another way)

3.

6 parts

6.

8 parts

Name _____

What's My Rule?

This is UDRF. UDRF has a built-in computer system. When you put a number in, it sends a number out. Figure out UDRF's computer's secret rule for each table. Write the missing numbers in the table. Then write the rule.

In	Out
200	300
53	153
327	427
13	
9	
18	

The rule is _____.

In	Out
455	465
18	28
30	40
273	
6	
120	

The rule is _____.

In	Out
120	100
63	43
240	220
32	
324	
26	

The rule is _____.

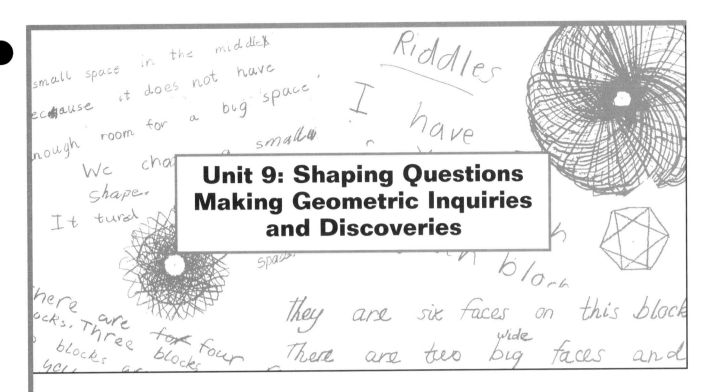

Unit 9: Shaping Questions Making Geometric Inquiries and Discoveries

Thinking Questions

How can you describe differently shaped blocks? How can you draw geometric shapes when you can't see all sides? Are there ways to build shapes by putting other shapes together?

Investigations

In this MathLand unit, you will answer these questions and learn to draw, build and talk about three-dimensional geometric shapes.

Real-World Math

Explore your house and neighborhood to find shapes that make up familiar objects. Look at tables, chairs, and other furniture to find the shapes of the geoblocks and Pattern Blocks. How can you describe and record the shapes you see?

Math Vocabulary

You will be using these new words to talk about shapes.

A **face** of a solid figure is one of its surfaces.

Example: All the faces of this shape are rectangular.

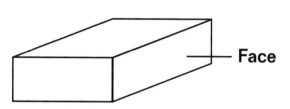

Face

To **rotate** something means to turn it.

These **shapes** are found in a set of Pattern Blocks.

triangle

square

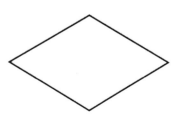

rhombus

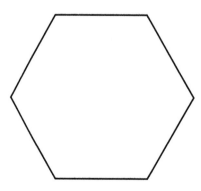

hexagon

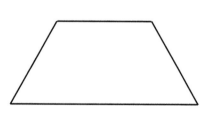

trapezoid

Word Practice

Practice writing the math words on the lines below.

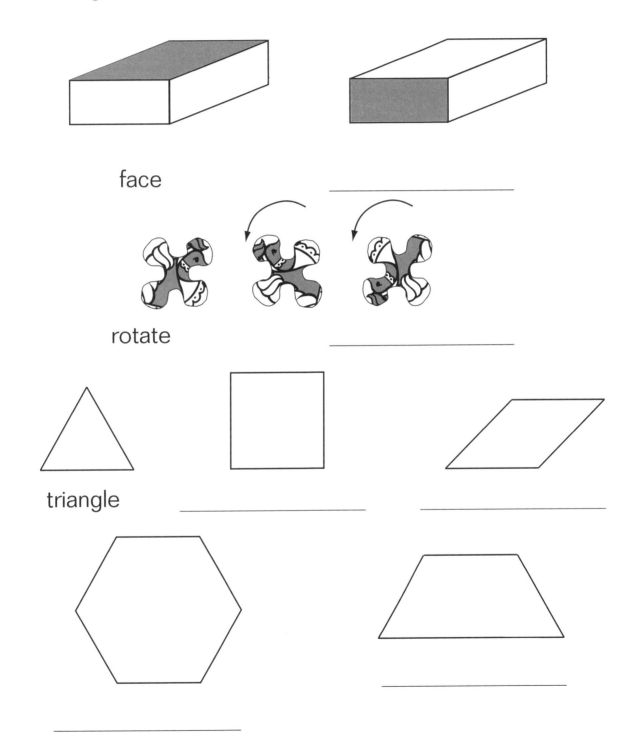

face

_____

rotate

_____

triangle

_____   _____

_____   _____

1

Write the Answers

$$170$$
$$+130$$

$$170$$
$$+140$$

Tell how you know.

2

True or False?

6 + 5 has the same answer as 9 + 3.

Prove it.

3

How Many Leaves?

Marc raked 34 leaves into a pile.
The wind blew away 15 of them.
Marc raked 7 more leaves into his pile.

How many leaves were in his pile then?

Show your thinking.

4

The Answer Is 200

Write 8 equations that have this answer. Can you think of more? Try it!

Write the Answer

28 + 13 = ___

Tell how you know.

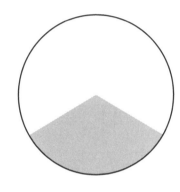

Choose the Answer

How much of the circle is shaded?

○ $\frac{1}{6}$

○ $\frac{1}{3}$

○ $\frac{1}{4}$

○ $\frac{1}{2}$

Tell how you know.

True or False?

8 quarters make $2.00.

Prove it.

How Much?

How much is ten plus eight, take away nine, plus two?

Show your thinking.

PARENT NOTE:
Support your child's natural inclination to take care of the big numbers first when adding and subtracting (rather than to "start with the ones"). This models successful strategies for estimation and mental arithmetic.

1

Write the Answer

3
18
2
1
9
+ 7
___

Tell how you know.

2

How Many?

How many are 10 tens?

Use pictures, words, or numbers to explain your thinking.

3

Count Backward

Which list of numbers is not correct?

A   100, 98, 97, 96, 95

B   44, 43, 42, 41, 40

C   12, 11, 10, 9, 8

D   50, 49, 48, 47, 46

Explain how you know.

4

True or False?

886 comes between 888 and 890.

Prove it.

What Comes Between?

Write the missing numbers.

1. 282 _____ _____ _____ 286

2. 311 _____ _____ _____ 315

3. 400 _____ _____ _____ 404

4. 199 _____ _____ _____ 203

5. 288 _____ _____ _____ 292

6. 447 _____ _____ _____ 451

What's My Rule?

This is UDRF. UDRF has a built-in computer system. When you put a number in, it sends a number out. Figure out UDRF's computer's secret rule for each table. Write the missing numbers in the table. Then write the rule.

In

Out

In	Out
120	107
32	19
473	460
20	
57	
284	

The rule is _____.

In	Out
341	353
118	130
162	174
10	
138	
299	

The rule is _____.

In	Out
27	18
498	489
59	50
20	
207	
86	

The rule is _____.

▼ PARENT NOTE:
Children who learn to make sense of arithmetic gain a strong foundation for the study of mathematics.
Children use their number sense and their logical reasoning skills to solve the problems in *Skill Power*.

1 Write the Answer

20
42
10
15
+ 5
_____

Tell how you know.

2 Recycling

Midori recycled 47 cans.
The next day she recycled 39 cans.
Then she recycled 27 cans, and after that 51 cans.

How many cans did she recycle in all?

Show your thinking.

3 What Makes $1.00?

Draw 5 coins that together make $1.00.

4 Choose the Answer

Which number comes between 1010 and 1012?

A   1011

B   1002

C   1001

D   1101

Explain how you know.

1

Write the Answers

225   250
+26   +26

Tell how you know.

2

True or False?

11 is half of 22.

Prove it.

3

Egg Cartons

You have 36 eggs.
A carton holds 12 eggs.

How many cartons will you need to hold all the eggs?

Show your thinking.

4

The Answer Is 318

Write 9 equations that have this answer.

1 Write the Answer

55 − 9 = ___

Tell how you know.

2 Choose the Answer

Which is equal to 100?

A   250 − 99

B   35 + 50 + 35

C   175 − 75

D   25 + 35 + 35

3 True or False?

Four hundred plus
four hundred equals
eight hundred.

Prove it.

4 All Fall Down!

14 children each have a
scrape on one knee.
The teacher has only
8 bandages.

How many scrapes will not
be covered?

Show your thinking.

How Many Do You See?

How many squares do you see?

Hint: The squares may be different sizes.

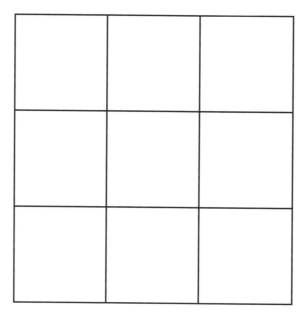

_____ squares in all

What's My Rule?

This is UDRF. UDRF has a built-in computer system. When you put a number in, it sends a number out. Figure out UDRF's computer's secret rule for each table. Write the missing numbers in the table. Then write the rule.

In

Out

In	Out
72	36
124	88
440	404
50	
96	
44	

The rule is _____ .

In	Out
118	124
12	18
354	360
75	
54	
133	

The rule is _____ .

In	Out
52	100
120	168
61	109
11	
414	
233	

The rule is _____ .

Write the Answer

$$\begin{array}{r} 63 \\ -24 \\ \hline \end{array}$$

Tell how you know.

Garden Planting

Amy planted 81 plants in equal rows of 9 in each row.

Show how the garden looked.

Use pictures, words, or numbers to explain your thinking.

Choose the Answer

Which time is closest to what the clock says?

○ 3:20

○ 3:25

○ 3:10

○ 3:00

Explain how you know.

True or False?

The number just before 1000 is 998.

Prove it.

PARENT NOTE:
Children who are encouraged to think logically about computations most often work from left to right, rather than starting from "the ones." This is a natural tendency that shows good thinking about the number system.

1. Write the Answer

19 + 27 = ___

Tell how you know.

2. How Many Counters?

Ben started a game with
20 counters.
Then he had to put
11 back.
On his next turn, he took
8 more.

How many counters did he
have then?

Show your thinking.

3. How Many?

How many tens are there
in 200?

Use pictures, words, or
numbers to explain your
thinking.

4. Choose the Answer

What part of 60 is 30?

A $\frac{1}{3}$

B $\frac{1}{5}$

C $\frac{1}{2}$

D $\frac{1}{4}$

Explain how you know.

Write the Answer

124
+ 7

Tell how you know.

True or False?

One fourth of this square is shaded.

Prove it.

Rides at the Park

12 rides at the park
were scary.
13 rides were funny.
15 were silly.
7 were for little children.

How many rides were
not scary?

Show your thinking.

What If?

There are 15 flowers in a
row.

Every third flower is red.
How many flowers are red?

Use pictures, words, or
numbers to explain your
thinking.

Shapes

1. Draw a shape having 3 sides.

2. Draw a shape having 4 sides.

3. Draw a shape having 6 sides.

4. Draw a shape having 4 sides.
Make 3 sides the same length and 1 side longer.

Can you write the names of your shapes? Try it!

What's My Rule?

This is UDRF. UDRF has a built-in computer system. When you put a number in, it sends a number out. Figure out UDRF's computer's secret rule for each table. Write the missing numbers in the table. Then write the rule.

In

Out

In	Out
5	307
110	412
28	330
177	
63	
39	

The rule is _____ .

In	Out
30	45
445	460
108	123
27	
222	
6	

The rule is _____ .

In	Out
169	19
257	107
400	250
191	
162	
180	

The rule is _____ .

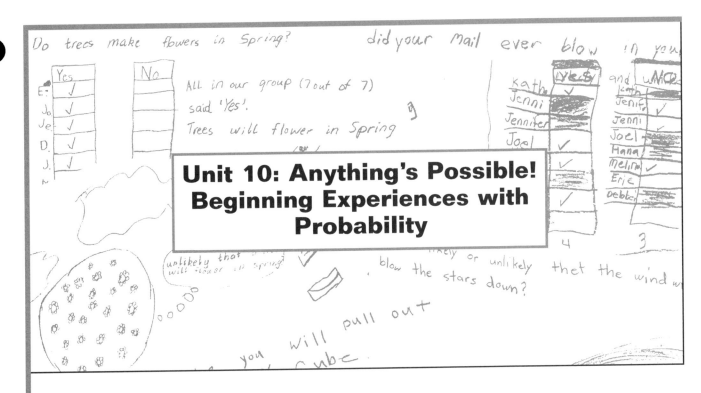

Thinking Questions

Is it likely or unlikely that most children in your class ride the bus to school? Is it likely or unlikely most children bring lunch from home? Can you know what's in a bag without looking inside?

Investigations

In this MathLand unit, you will be predicting whether something is likely or unlikely to happen. You will collect data by asking your classmates questions. You will use this survey to help you predict events. You also will practice how to predict possible number combinations.

Real-World Math

Surveys help people know what other people think and feel. What kind of information would you like to get by doing a survey of family or neighbors?

Math Vocabulary

You will be using these new words to talk about chances.

Something is **likely** if it is common or frequent.
Something is **unlikely** if it is unusual or infrequent.

Example: It is likely that the striped pants belong to a child.

It is unlikely that the shirt with stars belongs to a child.

A **survey** is a way of gathering information from many people.
You ask a question and record the answers you get.

Example: Sung used a survey to find out about his friends' families.

How many people are in your family?

Hanan	5
Robert	2
Ada	6

A **sum** is what you get when you add numbers together.

Example: The sums shown to the right are 6, 12, and 14.

2 + 4 = ⑥

6 + 6 = ⑫

7 + 7 = ⑭

Name _____

Word Practice

Practice writing the math words on the lines below.

likely

_____

unlikely

_____

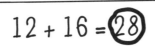

survey

_____

$$12 + 16 = 28 \qquad 17 + 20 = 37$$

sum

_____

1

Write the Answers

$136 - 7 =$ _____

$142 - 3 =$ _____

$168 - 9 =$ _____

Tell how you know.

2

Choose the Answer

There are 16 apples in 2 equal groups. How many are in each group?

A 4   C 5

B 8   D 6

Explain how you know.

3

True or False?

$8 + 3 = 11$ and $11 - 3 = 9$ are both true facts.

Prove it.

4

How Many Jars?

Eva had some jelly jars. She lined them up in 4 rows of 4 jars each.

How many jars did she have?

Show your thinking.

Write the Answer

$$24$$
$$+18$$

Tell how you know.

How to Make $1.00

Draw 7 coins that together make $1.00.

Choose the Answer

Which number is closest to $19 + 21$?

A   32

B   50

C   25

D   45

Explain how you know.

True or False?

$0.90 + $0.20 = $1.10

Prove it.

Name _____

1

Write the Answer

$127 - 115 = $ ___

Tell how you know.

2

How Many Peanuts?

Nate had 14 peanuts.
He put them in 2 equal groups.
He added 1 peanut to one of the groups.

How many peanuts were in the larger group?

Show your thinking.

3

The Answer Is 264

Write 10 equations that have this answer.

4

Choose the Answer

If 21 cookies are put into 3 equal groups, how many will be in each group?

○ 7

○ 6

○ 3

○ 4

Explain how you know.

What Is Your Answer?

Mikiko got this answer.

$$
\begin{array}{r}
17 \\
+18 \\
\hline
25
\end{array}
$$

Write your answer. _____

Did you get the same answer as Mikiko? _____

Write about how you solved the problem. Remember to tell about your thinking.

What's My Rule?

This is UDRF. UDRF has a built-in computer system. When you put a number in, it sends a number out. Figure out UDRF's computer's secret rule for each table. Write the missing numbers in the table. Then write the rule.

In

Out

In	Out
45	35
564	554
19	9
110	
83	
267	

The rule is _____ .

In	Out
3	273
112	382
87	357
204	
29	
228	

The rule is _____ .

In	Out
455	555
126	226
284	384
103	
299	
377	

The rule is _____ .

1

Write the Answers

102   102
+12   +18
—————   —————

Tell how you know.

2

True or False?

4 egg cartons of 12 eggs each make 48 eggs in all.

Prove it.

3

Logging

The loggers cut 74 trees one week.
The next week they cut 164 trees.
After that they cut 58 trees.

How many trees did they cut in all?

Show your thinking.

4

The Answer Is 250

Write 5 addition and 5 subtraction equations that have this answer.

1

Write the Answer

123 + 47 = _____

Tell how you know.

2

Choose the Answer

What number comes just before 780?

A   781

B   785

C   779

D   770

Explain how you know.

3

True or False?

If 60 books are piled in 4 equal groups, there will be 12 books in each pile.

Prove it.

4

Cereal with Raisins

You have 30 raisins and 6 bowls of cereal.

How many raisins do you put in each bowl?

Remember to put the same number of raisins in each bowl.

Show your thinking.

1

Write the Answer

144
− 15

Tell how you know.

2

The Answer Is 300

Write at least 9 equations that have this answer.

3

Choose the Answer

There are 4 cookies to share equally among 8 children.

What part of a cookie would each child get?

A $\frac{1}{4}$ C $\frac{1}{4}$

B $\frac{1}{5}$ D $\frac{1}{2}$

Show your thinking.

4

True or False?

3 quarters, 2 dimes, and 1 nickel make $1.05.

Prove it.

▼ **PARENT NOTE:**
A good strategy for solving one problem may not be as good for another problem. Children who are able to handle numbers in many ways think about the particular numbers in a problem to decide the strategy they will use.

How Many Ways?

How many different ways can you get from school to home? Draw the ways.

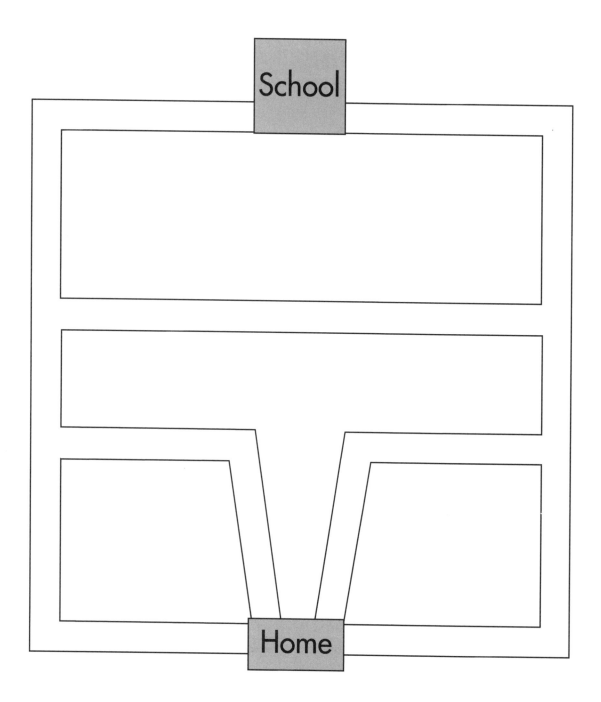

What's My Rule?

This is UDRF. UDRF has a built-in computer system. When you put a number in, it sends a number out. Figure out UDRF's computer's secret rule for each table. Write the missing numbers in the table. Then write the rule.

In	Out
36	55
150	169
7	26
300	
41	
11	

The rule is _____ .

In	Out
117	127
12	22
90	100
481	
375	
6	

The rule is _____ .

In	Out
57	13
250	206
144	100
80	
454	
88	

The rule is _____ .

What's My Rule?

This is UDRF. UDRF has a built-in computer system. When you put a number in, it sends a number out. Figure out UDRF's computer's secret rule for each table. Write the missing numbers in the table. Then write the rule.

In	Out
56	34
437	415
39	17
111	
90	
241	

The rule is _____ .

In	Out
92	31
84	23
426	365
70	
183	
235	

The rule is _____ .

In	Out
64	84
436	456
271	291
150	
4	
323	

The rule is _____ .

What's My Rule?

This is UDRF. UDRF has a built-in computer system. When you put a number in, it sends a number out. Figure out UDRF's computer's secret rule for each table. Write the missing numbers in the table. Then write the rule.

In	Out
100	17
296	213
88	5
484	
191	
323	

The rule is _____.

In	Out
229	204
145	120
98	73
27	
54	
381	

The rule is _____.

In	Out
95	500
17	422
3	408
76	
24	
69	

The rule is _____.

"The Parade"

Name _____

The parade route goes from the school to the police station. The route passes each building once. Draw the route. Then write a number from 1 to 9 by the name of each building to show the order of the parade route.

A. ____ Library

B. ____ Post Office

C. ____ Police Station

D. ____ Pet Shop

E. ____ School

F. ____ Fire Station

G. ____ Bakery

H. ____ Grocery

I. ____ Bank

Bank
6

Library
5

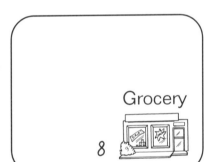
Grocery
8

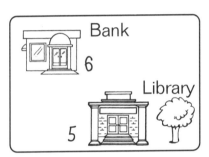
Bakery
7

Fire Station
4

9
Police Station

Post Office
3

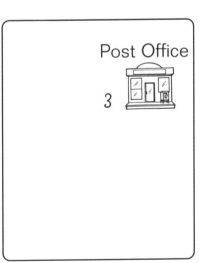
Pet Store
2

School
1

Six friends from the school are building a float.
They made a chart about the flowers that they will use.
Read the chart. Fill in the bubble next to the correct answer.

mums	150
tulips	275
lilies	100
daisies	225
roses	

1. The friends decided to change the design on the float.
Now they need 255 daisies. How many more is that than the
number in the chart?

○ 30   ○ 35   ○ 40

2. The mums and the tulips will be delivered from the nursery
first. How many flowers will be in that delivery?

○ 325   ○ 425   ○ 250

3. The number of roses used will be 25 more than the number of
lilies. How many roses will be used? Write the number in the
chart too.

○ 100   ○ 125   ○ 325

4. The friends need to know how many flowers they are using
all together. Find the total.

○ 750   ○ 875   ○ 905

▼ **PARENT NOTE:**
As preparation for standardized testing, children try sample problems and discuss them with the class.
The focus of this practice is: "What is this question asking?" These are practice exercises, not a quiz.

● The friends who are creating the float are keeping a tally of the number of hours each person has worked.

Sarah	ЈНТ ΙΙ
Michael	ЈНТ
James	ЈНТ Ι
Terry	НТ ΙΙΙΙ
Rita	ЈНТ ЈНТ ΙΙΙ
Tomio	ЈНТ ЈНТ ΙΙ

● **1.** Who has worked the most hours so far? _____

2. Terry plans to work 4 more hours.

What will her total hours be? _____

3. Tomio has worked exactly twice as many hours as his best friend.

Who is his best friend? _____

Three band members are painting the banner they will carry in the parade. The banner is long, so they are painting it in parts. Look at the banner parts. Draw a line from column A to column B to connect the matching parts.

A   **B**

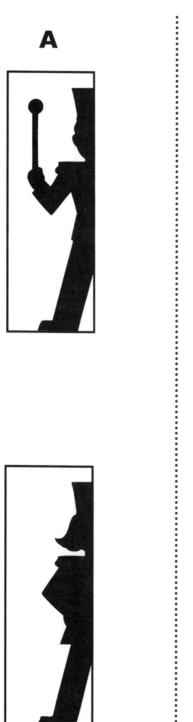

A marching band is passing by.

Sam tells Alicia he likes the musician with the tuba, the tall hat, and the boots the best.

Alicia says the musician she likes is different than Sam's favorite in one way.

Which musician could be Alicia's favorite? Ring that musician.

Name _____

Fill in the bubble next to the correct answer.

1. The marching band is passing by in rows. There are 10 musicians in each row. Sam counts 13 rows of musicians in the band.

What is the total number of musicians in the band?

○ 1310   ○ 130   ○ 131

2. The band also includes 4 baton twirlers and 1 drum majorette.

How many band members are there in all?

○ 1314   ○ 170   ○ 135

Many children are waving flags at the parade.

Look at the flag at the beginning of each row.

Look at the other flags in that row.

Circle the flag that has the same design as the first one turned in a different way.

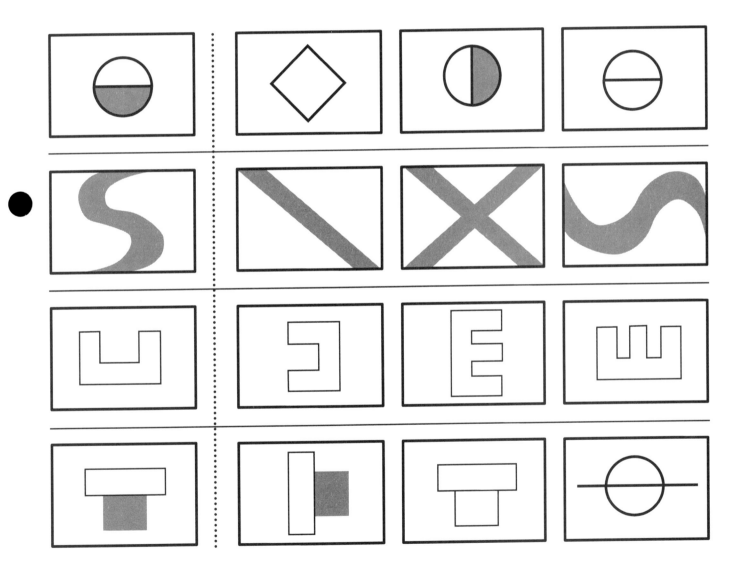

1. Sam has six quarters. What is one way he could spend his money on toys?

flags 65¢

stickers 75¢

balloons 40¢

_____

_____

_____

_____

_____

2. How many quarters would he need to pay with? _____

3. How much change would he get back? _____

4. Then how much money would he have left? _____

Many children are going to march in the parade.

The first child is holding a flag.

The children are lining up in this pattern:
  striped shirt, striped shirt, dotted shirt, striped shirt, striped shirt, dotted shirt.

Fill in the bubble next to the correct answer.

1. What kind of shirt will the ninth person on line be wearing?

  ○ dotted   ○ striped

2. How many children will be lined up when the fourth dotted shirt is in the line?

  ○ 10   ○ 12   ○ 14

3. How many times will the pattern repeat when 18 children are in line?

  ○ 7   ○ 9   ○ 6

Name _____

NATURE CENTER

"A Trip to the
Nature Center"

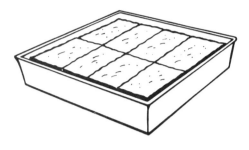
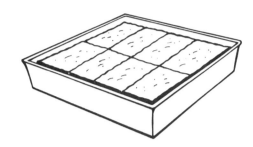
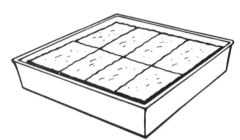
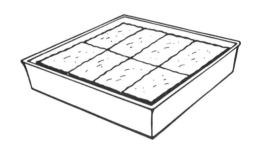

The class is going on a trip to the Nature Center.

1. The children baked 4 pans of brownies to take as a snack.
Each pan of brownies was cut into 8 equal pieces.
How many pieces did they have in all?

○ 28   ○ 16   ○ 32

2. Did the children cut each pan into an odd or even number of brownies?

_____

3. The class gave $\frac{1}{2}$ of a pan of brownies to the principal.
They gave 1 piece from the same pan to the school nurse.
How many pieces were left in that pan?

○ 3   ○ 5   ○ 2

4. Was there an odd or even number of brownies left in that pan?

_____

In the nature center, Amy wants to measure some feathers.

Use an inch ruler to measure the length of these feathers.

_____ inches

_____ inches

Amy says the top feather is twice as long as the bottom feather.

Do you agree? _____

Sam is at the exhibit about animals that burrow underground.

Sam plays a game using this spinner.

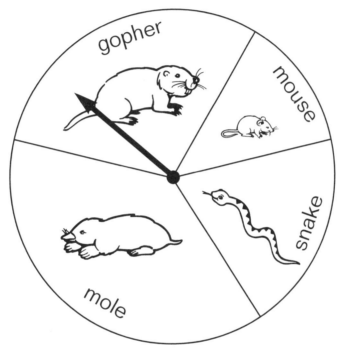

Each day many children play the spinner game.

1. In a day, which animal is the pointer likely to land on most often?

_____

2. In a day, which animal is the pointer likely to land on least often?

_____

Here are two stories . . .

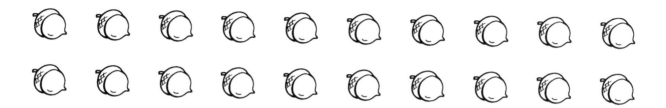

1. There were 20 acorns on a tree. Then 7 fell off.
How many acorns were left on the tree?
Write a number sentence to go with this story.

_____

2. There were 12 squirrels on the ground.
Then 4 squirrels ran up a tree.
How many were left on the ground?
Write a number sentence to go with this story.

_____

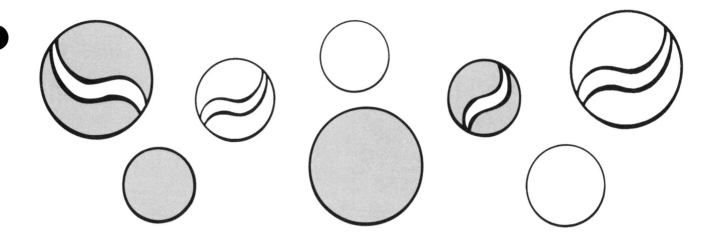

At lunch time, Kevin invites a friend to play marbles.

Here are the marbles Kevin has.

Sort the marbles into two groups.

Record each group in a circle.

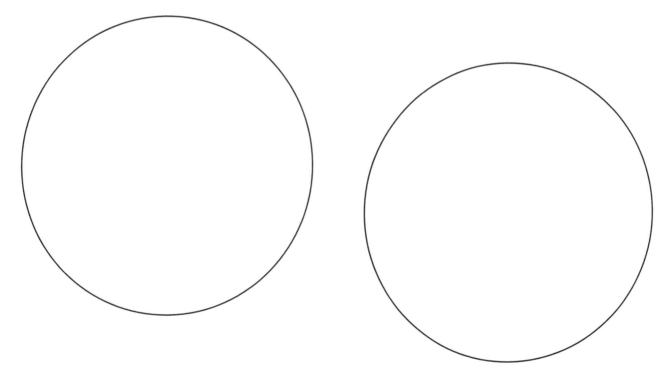

What is your sorting rule? _____

After lunch, the teacher says the class will leave the center at 2 o'clock.

Marcy sees it is now 1:15.

1. How many more minutes can the children spend at the center?

_____

2. The bus ride back to school takes half an hour. If it takes the class 10 minutes to get to the bus and get seated, about what time will the bus arrive at school?

_____

On this clock, show the time they will arrive.

Name _____

The children find another interesting activity.

Look at the picture at the beginning of each row.

Look at the other pictures in that row.

Circle the picture that is the same shape as

the first one, but smaller.

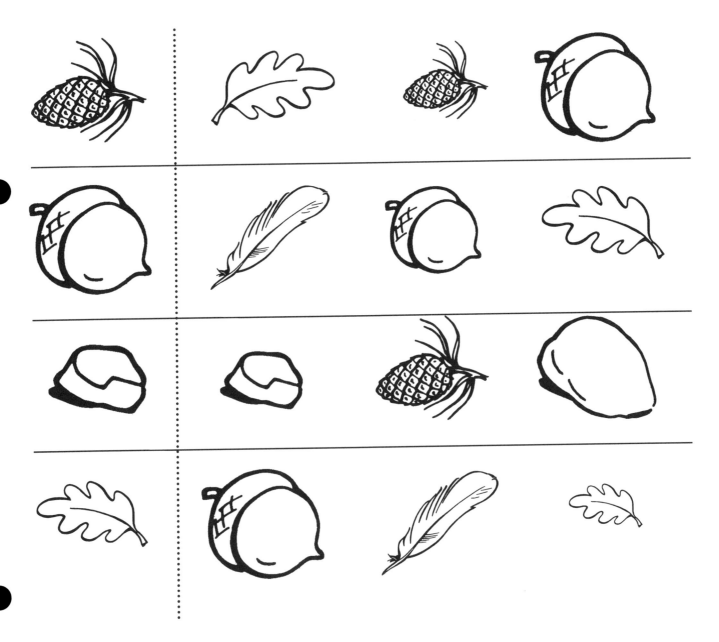

Marigolds	$.49
Bean Plants	$.50
Ferns	$.25
Herbs	$.33

1. Claire has nine dimes. What is one way she could spend her money on plants?

_____

_____

_____

_____

2. How many dimes would she need to pay with? _____

3. How much change would she get back? _____

4. What is another way Claire could spend her money on plants?

_____

_____

_____

With a ranger, some children go collecting around the center.

Then they use their collections to make patterns.

Alex's pattern is made of acorns and thistles:

1. How many objects will there be in the pattern when Alex uses a third acorn?

○ 4   ○ 8   ○ 7

2. How many times must Alex repeat the pattern to have

6 thistles?_____

to have 6 acorns? _____

3. What will the eleventh object in Alex's pattern be?

_____

4. How many times will the pattern repeat when 21 objects are used?

○ 7   ○ 8   ○ 6

Skill Power

Page 3
1. How many . . . ?
2. organize
3. sort
4. survey

Page 4
1. 4, 6, 8, 10
2. B
3. 12, Disagree
4. 4

Page 5
1. Answers will vary.
2. 10, 9, 8, 7
3. C
4. True

Page 6
1. 1
2. Answers will vary.
3. 11
4. A

Page 7
Answers will vary.

Page 8
5, 1, 2, 7
6, 5, 7, 8
9, 8, 12, 16
9, 0, 5, 7
10, 9, 12, 14
9, 6, 10, 11

Page 9
1. False (15¢)
2. 30
3. Answers will vary.
4. 18

Page 10
1. 10 − 5
2. False (1 o'clock)
3. 38
4. Answers will vary.

Page 11
1. 12
2. A
3. True
4. 13

Page 12
Answers will vary.

Page 13
18, 14, 17, 18
14, 9, 11, 15
14, 10, 12, 7
17, 16, 14, 17
9, 12, 16, 18
16, 14, 7, 8

Page 14
13, 14, 20, 13
13, 15, 20, 12
13, 16, 20, 15
10, 13, 3, 6
10, 5, 10, 5
8, 10, 10, 0

Page 17
equal
addition
subtraction
pattern

Page 18
1. Answers will vary.
2. 17
3. D
4. True

Page 19
1. 25
2. Answers will vary.
3. 10, 12, 14
4. 10¢

Page 20
1. True
2. 16¢, yes
3. Answers will vary.
4. 17, 13, 19

Page 21
10:00, 10 o'clock
4:30, four thirty
8:00, 8 o'clock
10:30, ten thirty

Page 22
1, 4, 10, 10
7, 9, 0, 0
2, 7, 7, 10
8, 8, 15, 16

13, 14, 18, 18
4, 7, 7, 14

Page 23
1. 8 o'clock
2. 54, Disagree
3. 5, 6, 7, 8
4. 8

Page 24
1. 10, 10, 10
2. B
3. True
4. 19

Page 25
1. Answers will vary.
2. 9, 11, 13, 15
3. 4
4. True

Page 26
Answers will vary.

Page 27
9, 6, 4, 5
19, 17, 14, 10
11, 15, 18, 20
18, 15, 11, 6
7, 9, 10, 10
17, 13, 8, 2

Page 28
1. 3
2. Answers will vary.
3. 2, 2, 2
4. D

Page 29
1. False (2 more)
2. 5
3. Answers will vary.
4. 12, 11, 14, 13

Page 30
1. 2 + 6
2. True
3. 6
4. Answers will vary.

Page 31
1. 2, 4, 6, 8, 10, 12, 14, 16, 18, 20, 22, 24, 26, 28, 30

are colored red.
2. 1, 3, 5, 7, 9, 11, 13, 15, 17, 19, 21, 23, 25, 27, 29 are colored green.
3. 10, 20, 30, 40, 50, 60, 70, 80, 90, 100 are colored blue.
4. 7, 70, 71, 72, 73, 74, 75, 76, 77, 78, 79 are colored yellow.
5. 97, 98, 99, 100 are colored brown.

Page 32
3, 6, 10, 6
5, 9, 14, 9
7, 12, 18, 12
9, 15, 22, 15
11, 15, 18, 15
9, 12, 14, 12

Page 33
1. 20, 18, 16
2. A
3. True
4. 4

Page 34
1. Answers will vary.
2. 14
3. B
4. Disagree (26)

Page 35
1. 26
2. Answers will vary.
3. 6, 7, 8
4. C

Page 36
Answers will vary.

Page 37
15, 12, 9, 6
14, 16, 18, 20
15, 16, 17, 18
15, 11, 7, 3
15, 13, 11, 9
15, 10, 5, 0